ATROPOS PRESS
new york • dresden

Performing the archive:
The transformation of the archive in Contemporary art from repository of documents to art medium

Simone Osthoff

Think Media EGS Series is supported by the European Graduate School

ATROPOS PRESS
New York • Dresden

151 First Avenue # 14, New York, N.Y. 10003

cover design: Hannes Charen

ISBN 978-0-9825309-0-0

TABLE OF CONTENTS

PART II
RELATIONAL AESTHETICS AND THE ARCHIVE: SENSORIAL EXPERIENCES BEYOND VISION TRANSFORMING AUDIENCES INTO PARTICIPANTS

Acknowledgments

I would like to acknowledge the European Graduate School for the stimulating discussions, seminars, and lectures, which I had the pleasure to participate in during the summers of 2005, 2006, and 2008. These intense intellectual exchanges celebrate the joy of thinking while combining the efficiency and speed of poetry with the rigor and slowness of philosophical contemplation, which the mountains of Saas-Fee invite. I especially want to thank Wolfgang Schirmacher for his challenging questions, encouragement and guidance. Diane Davis and Avital Ronell's generous insights, criticism and support have been invaluable for the conclusion of this research and the beginning of the next.

At Penn State University, I wish to acknowledge the colleagues who foster a cooperative and lively environment for the creation and discussion of art, media, and theory, among them Carlos Rosas, Micaela Amato, Don Kunze, Helen O'Leary, Gunalan Nadarajan, Irina Aristarkhova, Charles Garoian, Chika Okeke, and Sarah Rich. Many concepts in this book were discussed in my graduate seminars and I thank my students for their questions and their eager and open engagement with theory. Elsewhere, María Fernandez and Rainer Guldin read parts of the manuscript and provided encouraging comments. First from Chicago, and then from the great beyond, the late great Sir Robert Loescher continues to offer me inspiration and guidance.

I also want to thank the attentive staff of the following archives in which I carried out research. In Rio de Janeiro: the Projeto Hélio Oiticica, the Lygia Clark archive, and the Biblioteca Nacional; in Recife: the Paulo Bruscky archive; in Chicago: the Eduardo Kac archive; and in Berlin: the Vilém Flusser archive. I particularly want to acknowledge the continuous dialogue about art, philosophy and life across time and space with Flávia Schlee Eyler, Virgínia de Araújo Figueiredo, Gê Orthof, and Betina Waissman. I appreciate the encouragement and support received from my family, and above all, I want to thank my husband Stephen with all my heart, for his patience, his unconditional love and unwavering support. All qualities that make me value his criticism as my first reader even more.

I dedicate this book to the memory of my grandmother Zila, to my mother Therezinha and to my son David.

List of Illustrations

Figure 1. Eduardo Kac *GFP Bunny*, a public intervention in Rio de Janeiro as part of the artist's *Rabbit Remix* exhibition at the gallery Laura Marsiaj Arte Contemporânea, Rio de Janeiro, Brazil, 2004. *p. 19.*

Figures. 2, 3. Paulo Bruscky's archive in the Torreão neighborhood of Recife, Brazil. *p. 23.*

Figures 4, 5, 6. Eduardo Kac, *Free Alba!*, 2001 series. *pp. 34-35.*

Figure 7-8. Exhibition flyers from "History will Repeat Itself: Strategies of Re-enactment in Contemporary (Media) Art and Performance", curated by Inke Arns and Gabriele Horn at the Hartware MedienKunstVerein (HMKV) Dortmund, and at KW Institute for Contemporary Art, Berlin 2007. *pp. 46-47.*

Figure 9. Flusser archive, Universität der Künste, Berlin, Germany. *p. 89.*

Figure 10. Vilém Flusser's traveling library. *p. 89.*

Figure 11. Hélio Oiticica *Eden*, Whitechapel Gallery, London, 1969. *p.121.*

Figure 12. Nildo da Mangueira with Oiticica's *Parangolé 4 Capa 1* (1964). *p. 135.*

Figure 13. Paulo Bruscky "Xeroxperformance" at the Universidade Católica de Pernambuco-Recife, 1980. *p.147.*

Figure 14. Diagram of Eduardo Kac, *Rara Avis*, 1996. *p. 167.*

Figures 15, 16, 17. Eduardo Kac *Time Capsule*, 1997. *pp. 170-1.*

Introduction

Olhamos para o que não está e estamos no que não vemos.[1]

Katia Maciel

Artist's reflections on representation, vision and the invisible often alter the conventional boundaries of fiction and non-fiction. Topological spaces and the crisscross of gazes are found, for instance, in the symmetry of mirror images and in the placement of images inside other images. Dimensions that are usually kept separate in our common experience can merge through the contamination of space and time and ultimately between the realms of the living and the dead. Among classical examples are the visual puzzle of Diego Velázquez *Las Meninas*, 1656; the fourth dimensional perspective of Marcel Duchamp *Large Glass*, 1918-21; and the examination of the gaze and of the apparatus of cinema in Alfred Hitchcock's *Rear Window*, 1954; all pointing to the unknowable and invisible that continuously haunt our desire to see and to know.

This book focuses upon current disruptions of representation produced by contemporary artists, critics and curators. Their performances in, with, and of the archive are producing an ontological change—from the archive as a repository of documents to the archive as a dynamic and generative production tool. A few of these performances literally transform the archive into an artwork; others question its institutional boundaries; all contributing to change the archive's former stability, function, use, and meaning. This change in the archive's ontology, produced in part by the contamination between artwork and documentation, positions history and theory neither completely outside the realm of art nor entirely

---

[1] [We gaze at what is not there, and we are where we cannot see]. Katia Maciel "Margens da Palavra" in *Transcinemas*, org. Katia Maciel (Rio de Janeiro: Contra Capa, 2009), p. 426. Translation mine.

inside of it, but in continuous relays. Thus suggesting that history and theory can, at least on occasion, function as dynamic media.[2]

How do we approach artworks that change places with their own documentation? When artists employ historical archives as media is history affected? How are contemporary critics and theorists engaging the participatory nature of many artworks as well as the literal performances of the archive? Where does the body belong among the ubiquity of images? No longer able to maintain the neutral and safe spectator's position outside the space of representation, beholders, critics and historians alike are increasingly positioned as participants inside the artwork, who must author in real time and with all our senses the meaning of what we see and feel in multimedia installations.

The hypothesis — that the archive *as* artwork challenges the notion of history as a discourse based primarily upon chronology and documentation — no longer presupposes a stable and retroactive archive, but often a generative one. Consequently, the historicizing process of contemporary art is frequently *mise-en-abyme*, within multiple recursions of fiction and non-fiction, without foundations. And along with the body of participants, theory and history are increasingly included in the creative process.

Derrida's deconstruction of the archive in *Archive Fever*, as well as his examination of images, vision and blindness, particularly in *Truth in Painting*, and *Memoirs of the*

---

[2] Media is understood both as the plural of medium and as the means of mass communication, such as newspapers, magazines, radio and television. In relation to computers, the term media also refers to the materials or devices used to store or transmit data including hard disks, SSD's, floppy disks, CD-ROMs, and tapes. New media, more difficult to define, includes digital graphics, images, sounds, and texts, as well as the invisible connections that make them possible such as Wi-Fi.

Blind,[3] clearly inspired this book. Equally insightful and relevant were the performances of the archive carried out by contemporary artists, a few of which, I have previously examined elsewhere over the last decade. Therefore, this book is particularly indebted to the works of Brazilian artists Lygia Clark, Hélio Oticica, Paulo Bruscky and Eduardo Kac, as well as to the philosopher Vilém Flusser. The notion of topology, for instance, prevalent in the work of Lygia Clark as well as other Neoconcrete artists from the early 1960s, is a useful methodology to approach the increasingly fluid relations between artist's works, writings, and archives. And despite the growing international and scholarly interest in the works of Clark and Oiticica over the last two decades, many aspects of their works remain under-explored. Such is the case of the prolific textual production of Hélio Oiticica, especially from the 1970s, which merges avant-garde references from music, cinema, poetry, visual arts, architecture and design in multiple layers and languages. The examination of Oiticica as a multimedia artist *avant-la-lettre*, is only beginning to be explored.[4] Many aspects of Paulo Bruscky's conceptual oeuvre, especially his explorations of technology in the 1970s, still await to be fully explored. But it was the changing status of his archive of Mail Art in 2004, when it became an installation at the São Paulo Bienal, that prompted this book. Eduardo Kac is a visionary media artist and also an accomplished researcher and

[3] Jacques Derrida, *Archive Fever: a Freudian Impression*, Eric Prenowitz, Trans. (Chicago: The University of Chicago Press, 1996); *Truth in Painting*, Geoffrey Bennington, Trans. (Chicago: The University of Chicago Press, 1987); *Memoirs of the Blind: The Self-Portrait and Other Ruins*, Pascale-Anne Brault and Michael Naas, Trans. (Chicago: The University of Chicago Press, 1993).

[4] See Frederico Coelho PhD dissertation titled *Livro ou livro-me - os escritos babilônicos de Hélio Oiticica (1971-1978)*, defended in 2008 at the Pontifícia Universidade Católica of Rio de Janeiro, Brazil, is an original analysis of this material.

writer. He is among the few artists who can lucidly speak about aesthetic concepts in relation to other disciplines such as science, technology, communication and poetry. His artworks and writings emphasize the straight connection between art making, research and theory.

In my analysis of the works of these artists, who are difficult to categorize and even harder to localize given their trans-disciplinary, nomadic, and experimental practices, my intention was to avoid notions of self-identity. Theirs is a multidimensional network and dialogical thinking that cannot be fully analyzed by linear histories concerned primarily with issues of influence. Oiticica's use of precarious materials and processes, for instance, should not be equated with lack, scarcity, or "underdevelopment." He embraced popular Brazilian culture of the 1960s with the same conceptual rigor and sophistication that he first embraced the European constructive legacy in the 1950s and the rock counter-culture in the U.S. in the 1970s. He examined issues of artistic and national identity in many of his writings and interviews. In 1978, when returning to Rio de Janeiro after living for eight years in New York city, Hélio Oiticica, was questioned about how he perceived the ascension of Latin American art in the U.S.:

> I never liked to talk about Latin American art
> as an isolated category for various reasons.
> The first is that I myself would not like to be
> included in this category. Another is that I find
> it a very provincial approach. After all, Latin
> America is made up of very heterogeneous
> things and therefore this approach becomes
> very problematic [...] Would it be art made
> here? [...] I think Brazil has more in common
> with the U.S. than with other Latin American

countries. [...] Germany is closer to Brazil than Peru is, in terms of artistic languages.[5]

Like Oiticica, Lygia Clark worked for long periods abroad and she lived in Paris for almost all of the 1970s. Paulo Bruscky's work through the Mail Art movement has always been conceptual, international, and anti-hierarchical. Eduardo Kac also resisted labels that categorized his work in a reductive way: "I don't see myself as an 'American artist' or a 'Brazilian artist,' a 'Holography artist' or a 'Computer artist,' a 'Language artist' or an 'Installation artist.' I prefer not to be bound by any particular nationality or geography. I work with telecommunications, trying to break up these boundaries."[6] For reasons such as these, I chose to write alongside the artists instead of about them, also as a way to avoid using art as illustration for theory and vice-versa. I hope this book will contribute to close the gap between the two in the direction of more experimental, dynamic, and multidimensional media histories.

In this regard, Vilém Flusser had much to offer from the very beginning of his publications. His second book *A História do Diabo* [History of the Devil], published in Brasil in1965, approached history and the creation of linear time as the work of the devil. Difficult to categorize, the book combines philosophy and humor, science and religion, historical and post-historical thinking. By philosophizing in translation and without foundations, Flusser bridged languages, disciplines and cultures. A polyglot who fled the Nazi invasion of Prague in 1937, and lived in São Paulo for thirty years, before returning to Europe

---

[5] Lygia Pape, "Fala Hélio," reprinted in *ARS*, Escola de Comunicações e Artes (ECA), Universidade de São Paulo, n.10, p. 17. Originally published in the *Revista de Cultura Vozes*, Rio de Janeiro, ano 72, n. 5, p. 363-370, 1978. Translation mine.

[6] Simone Osthoff, "Object Lessos," *World Art*, N. 1, 1996, p. 18.

and settling in France for the next two decades, Flusser contributed in Brazil to the creation of a utopian nation based upon hybrid and mixed cultural identities. After 1972, he embraced exile — existentially, philosophically and ethically — as the basis for an analysis without foundations and a media theory that is ever more relevant today.[7] He has been both celebrated and criticized for his philosophical speculations and style of jumping across disciplines while ignoring, for instance, the traditional separation between the fields of art, science and technology. In one of his last essays published in 1990 he argued:

> If we abandon the idea of possessing some identifiable hard core, and if we assume we are imbedded within a relational network, then the classical distinction between "objective knowledge" and "subjective experience" will become meaningless. If intersubjectivity becomes the fundamental category of thinking and action, then science will be seen as a kind of art (as an intersubjective fiction), and art will be seen as a kind of science (as an intersubjective source of knowledge).[8]

Flusser's intuition that science, as a form of fiction, can be seen as an art practice, and that art making, as a form of theorizing, can be seen as a kind of science is among the methodological contributions to media theory embraced by this author. His iconoclastic picture theory is a product of such

---

[7] About the relations between Flusser and Art, please see the volume 08 of *Flusser Studies* (May 2009), which I organized: http://www.flusserstudies.net/

[8] Vilém Flusser, "*On Memory (Electronic or Otherwise)*", Leonardo, Vol. 23, No. 4, (1990): 399.

thinking, based upon the understanding of languages and technology as "gestures"—as apparatuses, devices, *dispositivos*.[9]

The following chapters explore issues of the archive, primarily through the phenomenological and participatory encounters with the artworks by these artists and theorists. It is divided into three parts. *Part one* — the archive as artwork — combines chapters that examine artists, curators, critics and theorists who contribute to destabilize the archive while raising methodological questions and historiography challenges. It includes a topological approach as a response to the crisis of art criticism, the examination of invisible aspects of visual culture, and Flusser's image theory along with a reflection upon his first three books published in Brazil, which remain to this day untranslated.

Part two — the archive and interactive art — examines the 1960s body-centered legacy of interactivity and audience participation of the Rio de Janeiro-based artists Lygia Clark and Hélio Oiticica. Their archives combine the preservation of original artworks, with the constant re-productions of these (a second collection of multiple "original" artworks), in addition to a number of blueprint instructions for the construction of new works, which were never built during the artists' lifetime. Thus, like their oeuvre, their archives transition towards the generative archive-as-database.

---

[9] The term *dispositivo* is commonly translated into English as "apparatus" or "device," which focuses on a more technical dimension. But the Portuguese *dispositivo*, like the French *dispositif*, carries the original meaning of the Latin *dispositio*, which in classical rhetoric was a system used for the organization of arguments in the sense of arrangement. Among Brazilian new media artists who are theorizing and producing artworks with the concept of the *dispositivo* and taking both Flusser's and Hélio Oiticica's legacy forward by deconstructing image projection and recording devices are: André Parente, Katia Maciel, Frederico Dalton, Rosângela Rennó, and Milton Marques. See also footnote 1.

Part three — performing the archive — probes artists' networks and the literal performances of the archive created by Paulo Bruscky's engagement with Mail Art and by Eduardo Kac's explorations of Telepresence and Bio art. The conclusion emphasizes the haunting dimensions of archives, which become more prominent as history, theory, and criticism are included among art's production tools.

Chapter 1

Elsewhere in Contemporary Art: Topologies of Artists' Works, Writings, and Archives

Figure 1. Digital street clock by Ipanema beach with image of Kac's 2000 *GFP Bunny*, a public intervention in Rio de Janeiro as part of his solo show *Rabbit Remix* at the gallery Laura Marsiaj Arte Contemporânea, Rio de Janeiro, Brazil, 2004. (Artwork © Eduardo Kac; Photograph by Nelson Pataro, provided by the artist)

On September 2004, when I arrived in Rio de Janeiro on my way to the 26th São Paulo Bienal, images of Eduardo Kac's *GFP Bunny*—his transgenic rabbit created in 2000[10]—

---

[10] *GFP Bunny* was Kac's second transgenic work, created in February 2000, with the birth of the hybrid albino rabbit "Alba" in a laboratory in Jouy-en-Josas, France. Alba contained the GFP (green fluorescent

were strategically placed throughout the city on three types of advertising displays: illuminated advertising signs mounted above digital clocks/thermometers displayed the enigmatic, fluorescent-green bunny [*Fig. 1*]; panels at bus stops announced Kac's solo exhibition at Laura Marsiaj Contemporary Arts in Ipanema; and constantly rotating displays in kiosks showed images of cultural events in the city, among them Kac's *GFP Bunny* and Bebel Gilberto's new CD album cover. A week later, at the São Paulo Bienal, Kac presented a transgenic installation entitled *Move 36*, which, along with Paulo Bruscky's apartment/studio/archive—one of the biennial's eight special rooms—,was identified by the media as a "must-see" presentation among the event's 135 works, created by artists from 62 countries. Interviews with both artists and images of their installations appeared in the major newspapers and magazines of Rio de Janeiro and São Paulo prior to, during, and after the opening of the exhibition.[11] I have explored aspects of

protein) gene of a jellyfish. She is normally white and glows green only when illuminated with a special blue light. Kac originally envisioned *GFP Bunny* as a three-phase project: the first was the creation of a new being through molecular biology; the second its public presentation in a gallery exhibition; and the third was the integration of the animal into the artist's family home in Chicago. However, after the French lab refused to release the rabbit as previously agreed, a worldwide media controversy followed, and Kac employed the media frenzy as material in the new phase of *GFP Bunny*, as exemplified in the photographs, drawings, and other works in his exhibition *Rabbit Remix*.

[11] Among many others, see Fabio Cypriano, "O Ateliê faz o artista," and Alfons Hug, "Mundo conceitual reflete crise da pintura," both in *Folha da São Paulo* (Folha Ilustrada), December 22, 2003, E6. *BRAVO!*, September 2004, featured a number of critical articles and historical highlights of all twenty-six biennials beginning in 1951. See also Maria Hirszman, "Bruscky leva seu ateliê a Bienal," *O Estado de São Paulo* (Caderno 2/Especial), September 23, 2004, H-14; Caroline Menezes, "Uma nova genética para a arte: Eduardo Kac usa genes para discutir relação entre ser vivo e tecnologia," *Jornal do Brasil* (Caderno B), September 30, 2004, B4; Giselle Beiguelman, "O xeque-mate cibernético," *Folha de São Paulo* (Caderno Mais!), September 19,

Kac's and Bruscky's multifaceted works elsewhere, and in this chapter I focus on the issues raised by Bruscky's archive and by Kac's new books, as well as the unsettled place of this theoretical and archival material within these author's work and in art institutions in general, including the writing of art history and criticism.[12]

A classic mathematical joke states that "a topologist is a person who doesn't know the difference between a coffee cup and a doughnut," since both forms belong to the same class of round objects with a hole in them—topologically called a torus—and can theoretically be transformed into one another. The use in art history of such a broad and uncommon term as topology allows one to go beyond the "vanishing point" and the habit of thinking about art in terms of the "projections" of perspective theory. "Points of view come packed with a full kit of ready-made subjects and objects, planes of representation, and radiating 'cones of vision.'"[13] Topology allows for linking near and far, up with down, in with out, in a paradoxical continuous space most easily understood by the classic example of the Möbius strip. Furthermore, topology underlines a reader-response theory. In a participatory paradigm, the artwork often unfolds in real time, and the viewer-reader must complete the

---

2004, 14-15; and "A Coelha Transgênica," *Veja Rio*, September 22, 2004, 43.

[12] Simone Osthoff, "Object Lessons," *World Art*, Spring 1996, 18–23, was my first article about Kac's work. My most recent is "From Mail Art to Telepresence: Communication at a Distance in the Works of Paulo Bruscky and Eduardo Kac," in *At a Distance: Precursors to Art and Activism on the Internet*, ed. Annmarie Chandler and Norie Neumark (Cambridge, MA: MIT Press, 2005), 260–80.

[13] Donald Kunze, "A Topological Approach to the Uses and Conceptions of Space, in Art, Architecture, and Everyday Life," unpublished paper, 2005, available online at http:art3idea.psu.edu/topology/index.html.

work's meaning. As the boundaries between art's inside and outside become less clear, meaning and authorship become more collective and distributed. In a participatory paradigm, for instance, completeness is no longer possible, desirable, or taken for granted. The artist's role as theoretician and archivist further disrupts boundaries between art production and its documentation, and therefore does the same to the traditional hierarchies between artists, critics, and art historians. Bruscky's and Kac's simultaneous practices of art making, archiving, and writing, as they move through various media, sites, institutions, and fields of knowledge, put into practice topological approaches to art.

Since the beginnings of their careers in the 1970s and 1980s respectively, Bruscky (born 1949) and Kac (born 1962) have often performed outside traditional art institutions and practices, forging complex relations between word and image, concept and medium, performance and documentation. Approaching art and life without regard for national borders or the categorical boundaries of traditional media, they have eschewed traditional venues, opting instead to invent new ones. Both artists were born in Brazil, and Bruscky has always been based in that country. Kac, however, spent only the first nine years of his career in Brazil (1980–88) and emerged in the subsequent years on the international art scene and the internet. Like other artists who engaged art with sites and knowledge from elsewhere in the cultural field, such as Robert Smithson and Hélio Oiticica, Bruscky and Kac have continuously drawn elements from art, technology, science, visual poetry, philosophy, and popular culture, promoting the blurring of distinctions among the artist and the theorist, the curator, the archivist, the historian, and the cultural critic.[14]

---

[14] Héctor Olea, "Versions, Inversions, Subversions: The Artist as Theoretician," in *Inverted Utopias: Avant-Garde Art in Latin America,*

Figures. 2, 3. Paulo Bruscky's archives in the Torreão neighborhood, Recife, Brazil. (Photograph by Léo Caldas, provided by the artist)

From Archive of Artworks to Archive as Artwork

Bruscky's studio, located in a two-bedroom apartment in the Torreão neighborhood of Recife, on Brazil's Northeast coast, has for eighteen years housed one of the most important collection of Mail Art in the country—fifteen thousand works— along with the artist's own oeuvre, books, newspaper articles, and other works ranging from artists' books and sound poems to films and videos [*Figs. 2, 3*]. Packed to the ceiling with papers, files, and all kinds of objects from brushes to kitchen utensils, this impressive studio-archive left Recife for the first time to be exhibited as an installation at the 26th São Paulo Bienal (September 26–December 19, 2004). Over the years Bruscky has made the archive available to artists, students writing theses, critics, and journalists. I went there for the first time in May of 2002 to interview Bruscky. Another visitor was Alfons Hug, the curator of the 26th São Paulo Bienal. "When he visited the studio," Bruscky recalled, "he came in, looked at every room without saying a word, came back into the living room, and proposed to exhibit the whole studio exactly as it was in the biennial. I did not expect that reaction, but I agreed, since my art and life have always been inseparable, and the studio-archive is clearly an expression of that. How do we give form to knowledge? In this space I make no difference between my works and everything else here, the archive, my library, my life. I spend more time here than at home."[15]

Bruscky was interested in research from an early age, but in the 1970s his interest acquired an added social and

---

[15] Paulo Bruscky, interview with the author during the installation of the São Paulo Bienal, September 23, 2004. Translation mine. All further quotes from the artist are from this interview.

political dimension, a sense of personal responsibility toward history and the preservation of a collective memory. "Each era has its own stories and histories. I was a victim of the dictatorship and had works destroyed by the police. Not only was my personal testimony important to preserve but also that of other artists involved in the Mail Art movement."[16] When Bruscky emerged in the art scene in the late 1960s and early 1970s, censorship and repression were commonly imposed by a military dictatorship responsible for one of Brazil's darkest periods of state political oppression, which began in 1968 and extended through the 1970s. (This era witnessed a wave of militarized regimes across Latin America, not just in Brazil, generally supported by the US government.) During this time, the practice of making art—especially experimental art—was a difficult and dangerous proposition. In spite of this climate, artists continued to resist authoritarian structures by pushing the boundaries of experimentation and the limits of public freedom. Bruscky participated in this and became a curator, creating in Recife a hub for the Mail Art movement. He later became a pioneer of fax art and xerox art (the name ascribed to photocopy art in Brazil). Not used to relying on public or official institutions for support, he developed instead a strong artists' network: "After all, the documentation of works made in the 1970s is in the hands of the artists." He exchanged letters and works with Gutai and Fluxus artists, among them Saburo Murakami, George Maciunas, and Dick Higgins, and learned about these movements from articles sent to him by the artists

---

[16] Bruscky was jailed three times, in 1968, 1973, and 1976. After 1976 he received death threats over a period of six months and was constantly followed by the police until he denounced this situation in a solo show at a Recife art gallery, making public the threats he had been, up to that point, undergoing privately. He was never associated with a political party, and his militancy was first and foremost cultural and artistic.

alongside letters and works.[17] He created a number of international events in Recife such as the *Artdoor* exhibition (on billboards across the city) with the participation of Christo, among other well-known artists.

Bruscky's archive is not only a seven-thousand-book library and information retrieval system containing extensive correspondence with artists, such as Meret Oppenheim. The collections of sound poetry and taped interviews range from Dada artists to an unpublished conversation with Hélio Oiticica. Bruscky has given the archive's large collection of comic books to his son, who is working with the medium. "Humor, puns, and word play are always present in my work. Humor is antityranny, antiauthoritarian," comments Bruscky, who has always taken the sliding meaning of signifiers seriously, and as part of the process, in bohemian fashion, hosts in his studio every Saturday a group of artists who join him in conversation and the drinking of a good *cachaça*.

An important cultural activist working outside the hegemony of Brazil's major cultural centers (Rio de Janeiro and São Paulo), Bruscky, who has never sold a work in his life, is experiencing a new wave of recognition from major museums and cultural institutions in Brazil.[18] Despite all the exposure and

---

[17] The Gutai group, founded in Osaka in 1954, included Jiro Yoshihara, Kazuo Shiraga, and Saburo Murakami. With an emphasis on performance, they reinterpreted Abstract Expressionism, then propagated this performance through the media, thus creatively misreading modernism. A similar creative response is found among Neoconcerte artists in Rio de Janiero in the late 1950s in relation to geometric abstraction. See Yve-Alain Bois's entry for the year 1955 in *Art since 1900*, ed. Hal Foster, Rosalind Krauss, Yve-Alain Bois, and Benjamin H. D. Buchloh (London: Thames and Hudson, 2004), 373.

[18] Bruscky's first large retrospective exhibition was held at the Observatório Cultural Malakoff, Recife, in 2001. In 2002, Bruscky's videos were screened at the Fundação Joaquim Nabuco, Recife, at the Cinemateca de Curitiba, Curitiba, and at the Agora art center in Rio de

attention his work is receiving, being part of the biennial was not new for him, nor did it excite him nearly as much as the precious rare books and catalogues he found on incursions into used-book stores during his daily walks between the hotel and the Ibirapuera park, where the Bienal pavilion is located.[19] A few days prior to the opening of the biennial, I asked Bruscky what might happen to the contents of the archive when it is exhibited primarily for its formal, personal, and idiosyncratic qualities, as a type of Merzbau. He didn't seem concerned with either the possible loss of content or the meanings the archive might acquire in this new context. He told me that, for one thing, the biennial docents were carefully instructed by the art historian who knows his work best —Cristina Freire—to address the content of the work as well as his working process. Bruscky's long experience with institutions, curators, and critics, as well as with their limitations, led him to trust that time will tell.

The question of the institutional location of the archive—physical, ontological, and historical—has become increasingly relevant to the writing of contemporary art history. As a powerful mediator between memory and writing, the archive constitutes a fertile territory for historical and theoretical scrutiny, especially for those engaged in writing the history of post-1960s art. In *Archive Fever*, Jacques Derrida, focusing on Sigmund Freud's archive, raised questions that foregrounded what Derrida saw as the inherent instability of representational processes. Probing which data belonged inside the archive and

---

Janeiro, accompanied by roundtable discussions. A comprehensive book about Bruscky's multifaceted oeuvre is Cristina Freire, *Paulo Bruscky: Arte, Arquivo e Utopia* (São Paulo: Companhia Editora de Pernambuco, 2006).

[19] Bruscky's work had been showcased in the São Paulo Bienal twice before, in 1981 and in 1989, when he was also invited to exhibited *heliografías* (works created with the technique commonly employed to print architectural blueprints).

which outside, Derrida asked, for instance, which letters and documents belonged to Freud's personal family history and which to his professional life and to the history of psychology. The deconstruction of the clear boundaries between personal and public spheres performed by Derrida in relation to Freud's archives slowly undermined common assumptions about origins, genealogy, authority, power, legality, and legitimacy. *Archival Fever* was prompted, as was my interest in Bruscky's archives, by the process of transforming the subject's house into a museum, and thus by "the passage from one institution into another."[20]

Besides Derrida's important examination of the archive, two other books have broadened issues of history, memory, and representation, offering useful alternative methodologies and approaches to archives. The first is Ann Reynolds's original approach to Robert Smithson's archive, which used a morphological methodology not very common among historians, but employed by Smithson himself as his working method. These morphological connections of eclectic material, such as images and written texts, diverse authors, disciplines, and concepts from popular and erudite culture, are "categories of thought and images that remain invisible to established hierarchies of interpretation."[21] The second book, written from the point of view of performance studies and focusing on inter-American cultural relations, is Diana Taylor's *The Archive and the Repertoire*, in which Taylor examines the

---

[20] Jacques Derrida, *Archive Fever: A Freudian Impression* (Chicago: University of Chicago Press, 1996), 3.

[21] Ann Reynolds, *Robert Smithson: Learning from New Jersey and Elsewhere* (Cambridge, MA: MIT Press, 2003), xv.

hegemonic power of text-based archival sources over performative, oral, and other ephemeral forms of knowledge.[22]

The experimental, concept-based, and often ephemeral aspects of contemporary art, which have only increased since the 1960s, producing fluid lines between work and documentation, certainly benefit from the issues raised by all three books, which pose relevant methodological challenges to more positivist approaches to documentation in art history and criticism. Bruscky's and Kac's works, writings, and archives put into play logical topologies that often escape the chronological and medium-based analytical methods of art history and criticism.

The Artist as Theorist

In September 2004, while Laura Marsiaj Contemporary Arts in Rio de Janeiro showcased Kac's solo show, his work was simultaneously exhibited at the Gwangju Biennale and the São Paulo Bienal, as well as in group shows in Chicago, Lima, and other cities. On top of this busy exhibition schedule, Kac was also finishing the production of two books, each collecting writings from a different period of his career. The first, *Luz & Letra* (thus far available in Portuguese only), is an anthology of his articles and essays written between 1981 and 1988 and published in the most important newspapers in Rio de Janeiro and São Paulo, along with an appendix of projects and sketches of the period.[23] Examining the broad field of visual culture in the 1980s, these articles have had a lasting impact. In their visionary

---

[22] Diana Taylor, *The Archive and the Repertoire* (Durham: Duke University Press, 2003).

[23] Eduardo Kac, *Luz & Letra: Ensaios de Arte, Literatura e Comunicação* [Light & Letter: Essays in Art, Literature, and Communication] (Rio de Janeiro: Contra Capa, 2004).

originality, they were early critical probes at the intersection of art, literature, technology, and popular culture. Written in an elegant, direct, and informative style, from a perspective both Brazilian and international, Kac's essays challenged established artistic values and venues, while opposing the label of the 1980s generation in Brazil as primarily a "return to painting" movement. In the preface to *Luz & Letra*, the art critic Paulo Herkenhoff, a former curator at the Museum of Modern Art in New York, stresses the importance of Kac as a theoretician:

> This book is a document of Brazil, which retrieves the decade of the 1980s—a period thought to have been lived under the tyranny of painting—as a moment of gestation of new ideas. Eduardo Kac is a precursor among precursors of media art theory [...] his action was always characterized by an intention to alter a system of hierarchies through the rescuing of artists and experiences.[24]

Kac's second book, with selected essays from 1992 to 2002 was published in 2005 by University of Michigan Press and titled *Telepresence and Bio Art: Networking Humans, Rabbits, and Robots*. In the foreword, James Elkins points out:

> This is an unusual book, because Kac has participated in the movements he discusses. He is an artist and also, at times, an historian. The combination is rare. A comparison might be made to Robert Motherwell, except that as an historian he was more concerned with surrealism than the art of his own generation: he separated documentation from creation in a way that Kac does not. Eugène Fromentin

---

[24] Paulo Herkenhoff, preface to *Luz & Letra*, 18 (my translation).

might be another example, and among near-
contemporaries there are Meyer Schapiro, Leo
Steinberg, and David Summers. It's a short list.
The closest comparisons may be to Moholy-
Nagy, or to Paul Signac, who wrote a history of
French painting up to and including his own
generation, or, though he's not much of an
historian, Frank Stella.[25]

Elkins is right in positioning Kac as a historian "at
times," because most of the time, the artist is a theoretician. In
his writings, the historical research is at the service of his
theoretical argumentation.[26] Kac's book articulates several new
concepts he has introduced, such as *telepresence art, telempathy,*
and *performative ethics.* Kac's work and essays about a new art
based on the networking of humans, plants, animals, and
machines not only examine current issues in science,

---

[25] James Elkins, foreword to *Telepresence and Bio Art: Networking
Humans, Rabbits, and Robots,* by Eduardo Kac (Ann Arbor: University
of Michigan Press, 2005), vi.

[26] Among Kac's contributions as a historian is the *Leonardo* editorial
project titled "A Radical Intervention: Brazilian Electronic Art." For the
most recent article of this ongoing series, Kac invited scholar Ruy
Moreira Leite to write a paper about what Kac saw as the artist Flávio
de Carvalho's pioneering use of the media. In 1956 the São Paulo artist
and provocateur de Carvalho introduced his summer garment *New Look*
in now-legendary *Experiences* for the press and on the streets of São
Paulo. In 1957 he introduced it on TV. Carvalho's garment consisted of
a short pleated skirt, a blouse with puffy short sleeves, a hat made of
semitransparent fabric, and fishnet tights. See Rui Moreira Leite,
"Flávio de Carvalho: Media Artist Avant la Lettre," *Leonardo* 37, no. 2
(April 2004): 150–57, available online at:
http://mitpress2.mit.edu/ejournals/Leonardo/isast/spec.projects/brazil.
html. Further editorial projects by Kac are: *Signs of Life: Bio Art and
Beyond* (Cambridge, MA: MIT Press, 2006); and *Media Poetry: Poetic
Innovation and New Technologies* (Bristol: Intellect, 2006), first
published as a special issue of the journal *Visible Language* 30, No.2
(1996).

technology, and culture, but also create dialogue with other artists and radical thinkers, often across time and space, who, like him, seek or have sought art's meaning in nontraditional places and fields of knowledge.

The meaning Kac gives to the word *aesthetics*, for instance, can be understood as both a topos (a theme) and also as a topology (either physical or logical). In the case of information networks, processes of communication can differ depending upon whether one is referring to a physical topology (e.g., the shape of a local area network) or a logical topology (e.g., the protocols that allow data flow within the networks). Kac's topological aesthetics emphasizes communication processes in real-time events and, since his employment of biotechnology as a medium, in the creation and social integration of new life forms. Didier Ottinger, the chief curator of the Centre Georges Pompidou, Musée National d'art moderne, Paris, compared the impact of Kac's redefinition of aesthetics to that of Marcel Duchamp's:

> Eduardo Kac's *GFP Bunny* set off shockwaves in the field of art comparable to those caused by Marcel Duchamp's urinal. Following the example of its sanitary forerunner, the rabbit's "prestige" grows in proportion to its invisibility. The animal, "created" by a French laboratory (the INRA at Jouy-en-Josas), was never exhibited in the public space for which it was conceived. On the other hand, its photograph did make the front page of the world's most important newspapers. Like the urinal, the fluorescent rabbit raises questions

that prompt us to redefine our own ideas and aesthetic criteria.[27]

There is indeed an uncanny juxtaposition between the publications of Kac's writings from the 1980s and his 2004 solo exhibition *Rabbit Remix*.[28] The show orchestrated the presence of *GFP Bunny* in the global media and a further intervention in the public space of Rio de Janeiro—the scene where the artist first started reclaiming public space in the early 1980s, while contributing to the erosion of censorship and the return of a democratic regime. The drawings and large photographs the artist exhibited in Rio de Janeiro continued the discussion of bio art in relation to science, ethics, religion, and family, issues Kac addresses in many forms beyond the gallery, such as articles and interviews, lectures and debates, and public interventions. Kac's remixing of the *GFP Bunny* icon, which includes the reappropriation of the media response to his work, both verbal and visual, employs the media as a medium [*Figs. 4, 5, 6*].

---

[27] Didier Ottinger, "Eduardo Kac in Wonderland," in *Rabbit Remix*, exh. cat. (Rio de Janiero: Laura Marsiaj Arte Contemporânea, 2004), repr. in *Eduardo Kac: Move 36*, ed. Elena Giulia Rossi (Paris: Filigranes Editions, 2005), 66–68.

[28] In *Rabbit Remix* Kac exhibited a series of photographs, drawings, a flag, a web piece, and a limited-edition artist's book entitled *It's not easy being green!*

Figures 4, 5, 6. Eduardo Kac, *Free Alba!*, 2001, from the series of six color photographs mounted on aluminum with Plexiglas, each 36 x 46-1/2 in. (91.4 x 118.1 cm), edition of 5, shown in the exhibition *Rabbit Remix* at Laura Marsiaj Arte Contemporânea, Rio de Janeiro, Brazil, 2004 (artwork © Eduardo Kac). Media coverage of Kac's *GFP Bunny* included articles in the *Washington Post*, *Folha de São Paulo*, *Le Monde*, *Ann Arbor News*, *Boston Globe*, and *Die Woche*. Kac incorporated the coverage in *Free Alba!*

A Topological Approach to Art in the Crisis of Criticism

In the course of the several decades that their trajectories span, Bruscky and Kac have forged through their practices the very space in which their work occurs. Unlike contemporaries who have relied on established media (such as painting) and whose work is embraced and circulated freely in acknowledged institutions (such as museums), Bruscky and Kac have often worked with new technologies and remote communication, short-circuiting the effects of institutional and market validation as well as physical distance in the circulation of their works. In their case the communicative act itself often constitutes the work. Thus, it is clear that the artists have taken a position that is critical of the institutional and discursive limitations that have not been able to incorporate and engage with their practices. This critique, which is often implicit in the material manifestation of their works, at times becomes explicit, as in the case of Bruscky's exhibition of his archive and Kac's books—both of which have I sought to highlight here.

Whether Bruscky and Kac perform criticism as an art practice or art as a critical practice, their multiple roles as artists, researchers, archivists, and theoreticians offer new topological approaches to the historicization of art since the 1960s. If there is a common agreement in current discussions of art criticism, it is the recognition of a general crisis as foregrounded by the 2002 *October* group roundtable "The Present Conditions of Art Criticism," by James Elkins's 2003 booklet *What Happened to Art Criticism?*, by Raphael Rubinstein's 2003 article "A Quiet Crisis," and by Nancy Princenthal's 2006 article "Art Criticism,

Bound to Fail."[29] Other critics have also called attention to the apparent paradox between the vibrant expansion of the global art market and the simultaneous demise of criticism in recent decades, pointing to the increased inability of contemporary critics to make value judgments, as art criticism becomes ever more informative and promotional than critical.[30] The relationships among art history, art criticism, critical theory, and literary criticism are more fluid than ever.

Judgment, in the sense of keeping up standards of "quality," however important in the past, no longer seems to be the most important function of the art critic. Whether critics write in a more subjective and impressionistic literary style or base their work on more rigorous theories such as semiotics, psychoanalysis, and Marxism, art's meaning and interpretation are increasingly an ongoing, largely "collaborative" process negotiated among multiple readers-viewers-participants and institutions, including those in the cultural industry. The role of the mass media and the art market in imposing the cultural value

---

[29] Rosalind Krauss, Benjamin Buchloh, George Baker, Andrea Fraser, David Joselit, Robert Storr, Hal Foster, John Miller, James Meyer, and Helen Molesworth, "Roundtable: The Present Conditions of Art Criticism," *October* 100 (Spring 2002): 200–28; James Elkins, *What Happened to Art Criticism* (Chicago: Prickly Paradigm Press, 2003); Raphael Rubinstein, "A Quiet Crisis," *Art in America*, March 2003, 39–45; Nancy Princenthal, "Art Criticism, Bound to Fail," *Art in America*, January 2006, 43–47.

[30] Barry Gewen, "State of the Art," *New York Times*, December 11, 2005. Gewen underlined the bleak state of contemporary art criticism by mentioning critics from Clement Greenberg and Michael Fried to Harold Rosenberg, Hilton Kramer, and, more recently, Donald Kuspit, who have lamented the gratuitous excesses and lack of restraint in art from the second half of the twentieth century. Even when enlisting more sympathetic critics of contemporary art, such as James Elkins, Arthur Danto, and the *October* group, Gewen observed they have not offered very positive answers to the question "Is the avant-garde running out of steam?"

of an artist is paramount but seldom if ever analyzed or critiqued.

It is not uncommon for critics to collaborate with avant-garde projects; examples include Clement Greenberg in relation to Abstract Expressionism, Ferreira Gullar and Mario Pedrosa within the Neoconcrete movement, Lucy Lippard in relation to Conceptual art and the women's art movement, Rosalind Krauss in relation to Minimalism and Postminimalism, Guy Brett in relation to the kinetic and participatory works of artists such as Hélio Oiticica and Lygia Clark, and Frank Popper in relation to new media art. For Krauss, an important function of criticism is "scanning the horizon for some new blip appearing on it."[31] Her statement can be understood in relation to the present and future of art, but also in relation to the past, which is always written from the present, as previously overlooked contributions are found and old legacies reinterpreted anew.

In these discussions, however, there is rarely a reference to the vibrant expansion and the formal or intellectual innovations of new media art, perhaps because the new media embrace a temporality and spatiality produced by the constant acceleration, overload, and complication of our natural and cultural environments. This development may be perceived to be at odds with the traditional focus of the humanities—but certainly not with the routine experiences of using cell phones, iPods, DVDs, ATM machines, e-mail, web searching and online commerce, to name a few common uses of contemporary technology that may be combined with watching TV and listening to the radio. Is this growing complexity good? What does "good" mean? Understanding the heterogeneous values and truths of our denser information environment and making sense of the paradoxical, unforeseen relations among these elements are in large part what art and critical theory do best, especially

---

[31] Krauss, *October* 100, 216.

when working together. Elsewhere in contemporary art, less-examined histories also suggest that art since the 1960s has continuously thrived in direct dialogue with criticism.

As with other artists who archive and write about the movements they participate in, the first impetus for Bruscky and Kac to document, to identify predecessors, and to cultivate a network of collaborators might have been prompted by the need to create a critical space for their work to develop.[32] As Bruscky's studio-archive has exemplified—changing its function from an archive of artworks to the archive as artwork—art and documentation may easily change places in his practice according to the institutional context in which they appear. And as we saw with Kac's *Rabbit Remix*, the artist has transformed the media and public reception of his *GFP Bunny* into the material for a new series of artworks.

The subtitle of Kac's 2005 book—*Networking Humans, Rabbits, and Robots*[33]— highlights a radical and hybrid connectivity in which, I argue, his books are themselves a constitutive element—a network hub.[34] Kac has often

---

[32] Other examples in the United States include Eduardo Kac, *Signs of Life: Bio Art and Beyond* (MIT Press, 2007); Donald Judd, *Complete Writings 1959–1975* (Press of the Nova Scotia College of Art and Design, 2005); Andrea Fraser, *Museum Highlights: The Writings of Andrea Fraser* (Cambridge, MA: MIT Press, 2005); Martha Rosler, *Decoys and Disruptions: Selected Writings, 1975–2001* (Cambridge, MA: MIT Press, 2004); Robert Smithson, *The Collected Writings*, ed. Jack Flam (Berkeley: University of California Press, 1996); and Joseph Kosuth, *Art after Philosophy and After: Collected Writings, 1996–1990* (Cambridge, MA: MIT Press, 1991).

[33] Eduardo Kac, *Telepresence and Bio Art: Networking Humans, Rabbits, and Robots* (University of Michigan Press, 2005).

[34] I expand this argument in the chapter "Eduardo Kac: Networks as Medium and Trope," in *Ecosee*, ed. Sid Dobrin and Sean Morey (State University of New York Press, 2009).

approached art institutions less as containers of culture and more as interface—as one more node of his networked ecologies. Such was the case of his telepresence installation *Rara Avis* (1996), in which the artist brought the internet into his gallery for the first time, to connect local and remote participants in the experience of a large aviary from the point of view of a telerobotic macaw.[35] Likewise, Kac's writings connect hybrid aesthetic elements such as language, light, and life, but can at the same time be seen at the crossroads of multiple institutional contexts such as the studio, the internet, the museum, the art market, scholarly research, and the mass media.

The juxtaposition of the publication of Kac's *Luz & Letra* with his exhibition *Rabbit Remix* reveals a direct relationship from the beginning of his career between his work, his critical writings, the gallery space, and the space of the mass media. In September of 2004, these multiple arenas were occupied simultaneously by the glowing rabbit icon, which also appeared throughout the city of Rio, continuing its four-year rapid propagation along with a controversy of unforeseen scale and speed.

Bruscky's archives and Kac's new books are more than collections of objects or texts to be consulted at a later time by an isolated researcher. The active and public diffusion of these artists' archives and books plays a direct role in the kind of art these artists make and the space in which the works circulate, as the works engage multiple institutional spaces topologically. The unique relations created between Bruscky's archives and Kac's

---

[35] *Rara Avis* premiered as part of the exhibition *Out of Bounds: New Work by Eight Southeast Artists*, curated by Annette Carlozzi and Julia Fenton at Atlanta's Nexus Contemporary Art Center, June 28–August 24, 1996. In 1997, *Rara Avis* traveled to three other venues: the Jack Blanton Museum of Art, Austin, Texas; the Centro Cultural de Belém, Liston, Portugal; and the Casa de Cultura Mario Quintana, Porto Alegre, Brazil, as part of the Bienal de Artes Visuais do Mercosul.

writings and their respective artistic productions—which for the most part have privileged real-time events, indexical processes, live interventions, and (in Kac's case) life creations—are examples of the complex issues involved in writing the history of contemporary art, in which the boundaries between work, writing, documentation, and reception are often fluid and include the multiple institutional spaces that artists help transform.[36]

---

[36] See Cristina Freire, *Poéticas do Processo* (São Paulo: Iluminuras, 1999), in which the Brazilian curator and art historian explores the uncertain place, both physically and conceptually, of the 1970s artistic production within the archives of the Museu de Arte Contemporânea of São Paulo, Brazil, which contains works by both Bruscky and Kac, among others.

Chapter 2

When Documentation and Memory Refuse to Settle is the Archive Alive?

> Because the essence of technology is nothing technological, essential reflection upon technology and decisive confrontation with it must happen in a realm that is, on the one hand, akin to the essence of technology and, on the other, fundamentally different from it. Such a realm is art. But certainly only if reflection upon art, for its part, does not shut its eyes to the constellation of truth, concerning which we are questioning.[37]
> -Heidegger

> The task of theory today is no longer negative. The job of media theory is to enable: to extract from what is and how things are done, ideas concerning what remains undone and new ways of doing it.[38]
> -Sean Cubitt

When artists perform the archive, and artists' archives are exhibited as art installations; when the mass media is used as a medium for art making and exhibitions re-enact historical

---

[37]   Martin Heidegger, "The Question Concerning Technology" in *Basic Writings*, David Farrell Krell, Editor, New York: HarperCollins, 1992, 340.

[38]   Sean Cubitt, *The Cinema Effect*, Cambridge, Mass; London: MIT Press, 2005, 11.

events by seamlessly combining documentary and fiction; when the past refuses to settle and nature's entropic processes are countered by a generative technology designed to upgrade and perpetuate itself—is history permanently undead? *Space time discontinuity*

In chapter one, I examined the examples of Paulo Bruscky's archive—containing the largest collection of Mail Art in Brazil along with the fourth largest collection of Fluxus worldwide, not including the artist's own works, books, newspapers, films, videos and tapes (exhibited as an installation in 2004 at the 26th São Paulo Bienal). I also analyzed the unstable boundary between artworks and their documentation in the aesthetic of the remix by focusing on Eduardo Kac's 2004 exhibition *Rabbit Remix*, which employed the mass media as a medium for art making [the work of these artists are further examined in chapter five and six respectively]. Here I want to briefly mention a few other examples in recent art and theory that have increased the fluidity between fact and fiction, thus further exposing some of the ghostly dimensions of the archive.

Of further interest to issues of memory, in relation to digital archives, is the notion of memory as computer storage being explored by Wendy Chun, who points out how memory as computer storage is programmed to self-upgrade in order to achieve an "endurance of the ephemeral." By comparing "memory" functions in humans and computers Chun probes media studies from a different angle: "What we must analyze, as we try to grasp a present that is always degenerating, is the ways in which ephemerality is made to endure. What is surprising is not that digital media fades, but rather that it stays at all, and that we stay transfixed as it regenerates."[39] Arguing against the

---

[39]   Wendy Hui Kyong Chun "The Enduring Ephemeral, or the Future is a Memory," paper presented at *re:place 2007 international conference on the Histories of Media, Art, Science and Technology*, November 15-18, Berlin, Germany.

notion that digital memory is stable storage, Chun points out that the upgradeable, regenerative and dynamic function of digital archives have created a crisis in documentation. Because digital archives depend on a dynamic performance to survive, they are literally alive, or at least undead, ghostly.

Mise-en-scènes of the Archive in the Exhibition *History Will Repeat Itself* and Slavoj Zizek's *The Pervert's Guide to the Cinema*

History Will Repeat Itself

STRATEGIEN DES REENACTMENT IN DER ZEITGENÖSSISCHEN (MEDIEN-)KUNST UND PERFORMANCE

STRATEGIES OF RE-ENACTMENT IN CONTEMPORARY (MEDIA) ART AND PERFORMANCE

Eine Kooperation zwischen dem A cooperation between Hartware MedienKunstVerein, Dortmund, und den and KW Institute for Contemporary Art, Berlin

9. Juni bis 23. September 2007 HartwareMedienKunstVerein in der at Phoenix Halle Dortmund

History Will Repeat Itself

STRATEGIEN DES REENACTMENT IN DER
ZEITGENÖSSISCHEN (MEDIEN-)KUNST UND PERFORMANCE

9. JUNI BIS 23. SEPTEMBER 2007 HARTWARE
MEDIENKUNSTVEREIN IN DER PHOENIX HALLE DORTMUND

In der zeitgenössischen Kunst der letzten Jahre lässt sich eine
fast unheimliche Lust an performativen Wiederholungen
bzw. Re-Inszenierungen historischer Ereignisse feststellen.
Die Ausstellung *History Will Repeat Itself* beleuchtet aktuelle
Strategien künstlerischer Reenactments und stellt die Posi-
tionen von 23 internationalen KünstlerInnen vor.

KÜNSTLERINNEN

Guy Ben-Ner (IL/D), Walter Benjamin (US), Irina Botea (RO),
C-Level (US), Daniela Comani (IT/D), Jeremy Deller (GB),
Rod Dickinson (GB), Nikolaj Evreinov (RUS), Omer Fast (IL/D),
Iain Forsyth & Jane Pollard (GB), Heike Gallmeier (D),
Felix Gmelin (SE), Pierre Huyghe (F), Evil Knievel (US),
Körpys / Löffler (D), Zbigniew Libera (PL), Robert Longo (US),
Tom McCarthy (GB), Frédéric Moser / Philippe Schwinger (CH),
Collier Schorr (US), Kerry Tribe (US), T.R. Uthco & Ant Farm (US),
Artur Żmijewski (PL)

History Will Repeat Itself ist das erste umfassende
Ausstellungsprojekt zum Thema Reenactment in
Deutschland. Es findet in der spektakulären, 2.200 qm
großen PHOENIX Halle statt, die der HMKV seit Ende
2009 nutzt. Die 1895 erbaute Halle steht auf dem
Gelände des ehemaligen Stahlwerks Phoenix West in
Dortmund-Hörde.

Pierre Huyghe, *The Third Memory*, 1999 · T.R. Uthco & Ant Farm: *The Eternal Frame*, 1975

Jeremy Deller, *The Battle of Orgreave*, 2001

Figure 7-8. History will Repeat Itself: Strategies of Re-
enactment in Contemporary (Media) Art and Performance, curated by
Inke Arns and Gabriele Horn at the Hartware MedienKunstVerein
(HMKV) Dortmund, and at KW Institute for Contemporary Art, Berlin
2007. (Exhibition flyer photo: Heike Gallmeier, War & Peace Show:
Minipanzerschlacht, photography, 2004; Graphic design by
www.laborb.de; courtesy of Inke Arns and the Hartware
MedienKunstVerein (HMKV) Dortmund).

Aside from the contribution of artists and historians, the
emerging histories of media arts are also being enriched by
contributions from curators and theorists. Such is the case of a
show that highlighted another form of remix—the uncanny,
contemporary attraction to historical re-enactments. Curated by
Inke Arns and Gabriele Horn, the exhibition *History will Repeat*

Itself: Strategies of Re-enactment in Contemporary (Media) Art and Performance [*Figs.* 7, 8] took place in Berlin in 2007 showcasing large installations by 30 international artists. The exhibition probed questions about personal and collective memory (often traumatic events that left their traces in the twentieth century's *mind*), while emphasizing the fluid boundary separating fact from fiction.

"Re-enactments are artistic interrogations of media images that try to scrutinize the reality of the images, while at the same time pointing towards the fact that collective memory is essentially mediated memory."[40] And to this end, by unveiling the mediated nature of collective memory, the exhibition employed history as a theme as well as a medium. The artists in this show engaged history and representation, trauma and truth, both individually and collectively. Multiple strategies towards historical events made the exhibition a conceptually compelling and visually vibrant examination of history with a proliferation of media that included film, video, sound, objects, text, and photographs all combined in various size installations distributed throughout the KW multiple-story galleries, from small rooms to larger spaces, some divided into multiple installations and others containing a single larger one, thus transforming the building itself into a powerful building of history and memory.

A first example I will describe is Omer Fast's double video channel installation titled *Spielberg's List*.[41] Fast explored

---

40   The sentence comes from the exhibition press release. *History will Repeat Itself: Strategies of Re-enactment in Contemporary (Media) Art and Performance* was organized by Inke Arns and Gabriele Horn for two German venues: the Hartware MedienKunstVerein (HMKV) at Phoenix Halle Dortmund: June 9 - September 23, 2007, and the KW Institue for Contemporary Art, November 18, 2007-January 13, 2008, Berlin-Mitte. The exhibition is also traveling to the Goethe-Institut Hong Kong in June 2008.

41   Omer Fast, *Spielberg's List.* Two-channel video installation,

the film set constructed for Spielberg's *Schindler's List* in Krakow—a section of a concentration camp built for the film.[42] Ten years afterwards, that stage site had fallen in disrepair and it is indistinguishable from other Second World War concentration camps surrounding it, and in addition, it has become part of the region's Holocaust tourist industry, as the "historical site" of Spielberg's film. Fast filmed it and sutured his own footage with excerpts from Spielberg's film, thus making it difficult to separate the two films and impossible to distinguish Spielberg's documentary-drama from Fast's altered version of it. Fast's footage also included interviews with many film extras that participated in *Schindler's List*. Projected onto TV screens side by side, their memories of the media event were further mingled by video editing, their memories of the Holocaust further distancing the audience from the original historical events by continuously layering them with multiple witness performances and narratives. Viewers were reminded of all the films that make up our collective memory of the Second World War and by extension of history, thus by analogy implicating other narrative forms, both documentary and fictional, scholarly and popular, spoken, written and visual, which mediate our collective memory.

A second example is by French artist Pierre Huyghe, whose film installation *Third Memory* typify his interest, neither in filming and documenting reality nor in building fiction, but

---

transferred to DVD, 65min., English/Polish with English subtitles, 2003.

[42] Stephen Spielberg's filmography includes three feature dramas supposedly based upon true stories. Such was the case of *Schindler's List*, 1993, based on the true story of Oskar Schindler, a man who risked his life to save 1,100 people from the Holocaust; *Saving Private Ryan*, 1998, also taking place in the Second World War; and *Munich*, 2005, about the events following the Munich Massacre of Israeli athletes at the Olympic Games.

rather in setting up a reality (such as a community "happening")
then filming this performance.[43] Pierre Huyghe, *The Third
Memory*,[44] is described by the co-curator Katharina Fichtner:

> *The Third Memory* was based on a legendary
> bank robbery, which took place on the 22nd of
> August, 1972, in Brooklyn, New York. John
> Woytowiczs robbed a branch of the Chase
> Manhattan Bank, took several people as
> hostages, and in the end was caught. This bank
> robbery was one of the first criminal acts to be
> broadcast live on television, and was seen by
> millions of people. Three years later, in 1975,
> Sidney Lumet's classic movie *Dog Day
> Afternoon*, in which Al Pacino plays the bank
> robber Woytowiczs, was based on this event.
> For *The Third Memory*, Huyghe asked the
> aging John Woytowiczs, if he would be
> prepared to talk about the event that had had
> such drastic effects on his life. On a simple set,
> a counter hall similar to the scene in the film,
> Woytowiczs re-enacts the event with a group
> of actors; he is as self-confident as the director
> of a detective film. The two-channel video
> installation connects this re-enactment to the
> original recordings by the television channels
> and scenes taken from the Hollywood film
> version. Today, the circumstances of the bank

---

[43]   Pierre Huyghe's statement about his working process in *Art
21: Art in the Twenty-First Century*, PBS DVD documentary series,
2007.

[44]   Pierre Huyghe, *The Third Memory* is a two-channel video
installation, (Digital Beta, transferred to DVD, 9:46min., 1999) part of
the exhibition *History Will Repeat Itself*, at the KW in Berlin,
November of 2007.

robbery in August 1972 are known to many people mainly through the movie starring Al Pacino. When Woytowiczs now re-enacts these events, the intention is not to correct a version falsified by the media, and finally to tell the 'true story.' With *The Third Memory* Huyghe shows the interplay between how history and recollection are determined by media and fictional images on the one side, and on the other how real life is influenced by fiction. In actual fact Woytowiczs modelled his behaviour during the bank robbery on Al Pacino's role in *The Godfather*.[45]

This ghostly spectrum of memory, traces, and remainders, present in history yet invisible until examined, is the focus of Jacques Derrida's deconstruction. Derrida examines hidden dimensions of images and vision especially in *Truth in Painting* and *Memoirs of the Blind*. His careful examination of signs, unhinging meanings in order to produce fresh and often subversive ones, is also observed in art's topological connections between the inside and the outside of the images' frame. Examples are Diego Velázquez's *Las Meninas*, comic strips like *krazy kat*, Alfred Hitchcock's *Rear Window*, and such paradoxical images are also present in short stories by Jorges Luis Borges.

A contemporary example of a theorist exploring a similar cinematic hinge between inside/outside the frame, while creatively and scholarly engaging documentary and fiction, desire and fantasy, is Slavoj Zizek in *The Pervert's Guide to the*

[45]   Exhibition handout from the website www.hmkv.de (accessed on April 30, 2008).

Cinema, directed by Sophie Fiennes and released in 2005. *The Pervert's Guide* includes some of Zizek's analysis of Hitchcock's films from his book *Looking Awry, An Introduction to Jacques Lacan Through Popular Culture*.[46] However, in *The Pervert's Guide*, Zizek and the director Sophia Fiennes offer a cinematic dimension to Zizek's scholarly criticism on popular culture. They employ editing and special effects, including the reconstruction of some of the original movies scenes, which they suture together with some of the original movie clips. Thus Zizek delivers his insightful cinematic and psychoanalytic critique from inside the space he is analyzing. The result is both entertaining and powerful as it amplifies the crisscross of original and fictional spaces and gazes, in which the critic/theorist is both inside and outside of the films he critiques. This paradoxical movement that continuously destabilizes the inside and the outside boundaries of each image, brings the original films closer to the audience and further implicates us in a topological movement—a chiasmus—which in *Looking Awry*, Zizek addresses through the notion of anamorphosis, a perspective that distorts images so that they only become clear from an extremely diagonal point of view in relation to the screen. In *The Pervert's Guide*, Zizek demonstrates, cinematically, the paradox of being both inside and outside of the fictional space, by literally crossing the screen boundary with the suturing of new and old footages—those of Hitchcock and of other film directors, with Zizek's own critical performance and fictional reenactments of the original fiçtional mise-en-scènes.

Thinking about Bruscky's Mail Art archive exhibited as an installation; Kac's exhibition *Rabbit Remix* employing the media as a medium; Chun's observations about the regeneration of computer memory; as well as Arns and Horn's exhibition

---

[46]   Slavoj Zizek, *Looking Awry, An Introduction to Jacques Lacan Through Popular Culture* (Cambridge, MA: MIT Press, 1997).

History Will Repeat Itself; and the "participatory" and creative performances of Zizek's and Fiennes' *The Pervert's Guide*—I believe histories of media, art, science and technology, rather than becoming a proliferation of case studies that seek to fix their place within a more established international art history canon, need to first and foremost critically engage with historiography and methodology as such, as media capable of topological performances of their own. Thus approaching history as a particular media with both limitations and potential. Media histories to come will neither forget nor become nostalgic for social histories of particular places, nor their cultural identities and heritages, yet they will approach them as part of our always already mediated collective memories.

The Non-Visual Within Visual Studies

Despite the growing scholarship and the increasing number of programs in the field of visual studies, art historian James Elkins has pointed out the common tendency to cite the same theorists: "Most writing in visual studies can accomplish what it wants to without citing Benjamin's dialectical image, Foucault's panopticon, Warburg's *Pathosformeln*, Lacan's *objet petit a*, Peirce's icon-index-symbol, or Barthe's punctum. An idea does not always become clearer or stronger by being linked to such concepts."[47] In *Visual Studies: A Skeptical Introduction* Elkins considers multiple ways of asking about what visual literacy is today. Without forgetting the methodological wealth of art history, he argues for an expansion of the visual studies, one "welcoming scientists from various disciplines, moving beyond pre-modern Western visuality and into non-Western art,

---

[47] James Elkins, *Visual Studies: A Skeptical Introduction*, New York and London: Routledge, 2003, p. 101. (Hereafter cited in the text as *VS*)

archaeology, and the visual elements of linguistics." (*VS* 41) Elkins proposes an approach to the visual that is less a body of knowledge and more a methodological inquiry—modes of framing, questioning and interpretation. He points out how many scholars continue to repeat the mantra that our culture is increasingly visual by reiterating W.J.T. Mitchell's expressions "pictorial turn" and "picture theory," as well as other common remarks along the lines of "the increased dominance of visual media," "the age of pictures," "the visual age," "the paradigm shift towards the visual," "the age of simulacrum," etc. (*VS* 131)

In contrast to the notion that our times are primarily visual, Elkins offers three arguments that are worth listing here. The first one can be summed up as follows: "as far as philosophy was concerned, the very twentieth-century French phenomenological and poststructural thinking that underwrites much of literary theory and theoretically minded art history was itself consistently nonvisual." (*VS* 133) Elkins includes as examples famous passages, such as Lacan's mirror stage and Heidegger's analysis of Van Gogh's painting in the *Origin of the Work of Art* and argues that they are not really interrogated in terms of their visuality. (*VS* 132)

The second argument he offers as argument that the century might not be primarily visual is based on Barbara Stafford's idea that we can easily understand fast and direct graphic design communication but are illiterate about pre-modern graphics, which were not meant for quick reading and decoding. Stafford argues that we cannot decode such slow images as the ones layered with all kinds of symbols by alchemists. These images, along with a wealth of non-Western images such as Meso-American paintings or Chinese paintings, no matter how widespread their meaning and their scholarship in other parts of the world, are mostly lost to our contemporary eyes. According to Stafford's argument, we may have acquired some new visual skills but in the process lost others that were as important.

The third argument against the belief in a widespread visual culture discussed by Elkins relates to the invisible dimensions of technology. He quotes Laura Marks: "'the period of visual culture is over,' she says, so 'it is ironic that all these programs in visual studies are starting up, just at the point where information culture, which is invisible, is becoming the dominant mode.'" (*VS* 136) This last argument points out the invisible but pervasive reach of information technology: just think how banks, governments and corporations know about our identity, consumer patterns, and preferences, as well as our financial status. The argument shifts the focus from the visual realm to the social and political implications of information technology and thus demands that economic studies and critical studies on networks, surveillance, design, and marketing be an essential part of visual studies.

In addition to Marks's arguments there is much in relation to the field of art and technology that is not visual especially in relation to nanotechnology and genetic engineering, which are further examples of the invisible and far reaching dimensions of the work of a few visual artists such as Eduardo Kac. Genetic engineering, networks, databases, the flux and overflow of information are not only changing the way art is being made and consumed but also documented and stored. These technologies are changing the way we understand documentation, memory, and archives, and thus, how we historicize contemporary art.

Many agree that visual studies needs to take into consideration the non-visual implications of images production, circulation, and reception. Siegfried Zielinski's media archeology, for instance, insists that media scholarship needs to be at the same time broad and long-ranging, yet capable of deep, particular and singular scrutiny.[48] Other media critics, such as

---

[48]   Siegfried Zielinski, *Deep Time of the Media: Towards an Archeology of Hearing and Seeing by Technical Means* (Cambridge,

Sean Cubitt call attention to a criticism that can be reactive and at the same time generative, even visionary. An example is Vilém Flusser's elastic thinking, which because of its unorthodox methodology and language, has been accused of being "imprecise."[49]

Among philosophers, perhaps the most thorough methodological scrutiny has been made by Jacques Derrida's deconstruction of Western metaphysics. Similar to Heidegger's philosophical inquiry into the meaning of Being, as that which presupposes thinking and is given prior to investigation—for instance in the question "What is..?"—Derrida scrutinized that which is not-thought in the text. In place of "Being" which Heidegger puts under investigation, Derrida puts the sign, thus exercising a deconstruction of language's formal authority and identity at the same time that he employs language in performing this critique. Derrida does not present knowledge, he builds a case by thinking about, through, and with language. Usually by following the etymology of certain words and of supplemental meanings found in alternative uses of words that he puts under scrutiny, as Heidegger does with the question of "Being." Derrida suspends meaning in the text in order to expose hidden meanings that are present/absent from the text. Thus Derrida proposes a difficult methodological operation, in which one must learn how to use and question language simultaneously.

MA: MIT Press, 2006); and Siegfried Zielinski, *Audiovisions: Cinema and Television as Entr'actes in History*, (Amsterdam: Amsterdam University Press, 1999).

[49]   Rainer Guldin, "Iconoclasm and Beyond: Vilém Flusser Concept of Techno-Imagination," *Journal of the Swiss Association of Communication and Media Research*, Vol. 7, N. 2, 2007, 67.

Alain Badiou: "Passion for the Real," Representation, Documentation

In *The Century*, Alain Badiou begins his methodological examination of the different ways in which one could define the twentieth century by asking: "What is a century?" and he answers in analogy to another apparently simple questioning: "I have in mind Jean Genet's preface to his play *The Blacks*. In it, he asks ironically: 'What is a black man?' Adding at once: 'And first of all, what color is he?'"[50] By employing a philosophical interrogation that questions common assumptions in both language and history, Badiou asks which significant events should one privilege? In offering at least three frames of reference for marking the beginning and end of the century, Badiou forges a fresh analytical model that is simultaneously scholarly and activist. Instead of assuming "neutrality" and keeping a "proper" historical distance from his object of study—in this case the twentieth century avant-gardes— Badiou clearly expresses his point of view: his admiration for the twentieth-century avant-gardes' utopian and generative ideas, which in spite of, or perhaps precisely because they are inseparable from the violence, politics and wars that characterized the twentieth century, continue to pose central questions about representation in art, theory, and politics.

Badiou's *The Century* contrasts numerous postmodern writings about visual culture, which are simply reactive and critical of Modernism in their desire to go beyond its accomplishments and contradictions. Instead, he insists upon the need to come to terms with the central challenges and concerns of the twentieth century, if we are to deepen our understanding of art, theory, and politics in the twentieth-first century. To this end, Badiou enlists art and poetry and explores the twentieth

---

50   Alain Badiou, *The Century*, Canbridge: Polity, 2007, 1.

century in terms of its obsessive themes, highlighting among them "the passion for the real": "The real, as all key players of the century recognize, is the source of both horror and enthusiasm, simultaneously lethal and creative,"[51] especially, Badiou observed, because the century has unfolded under the paradigm of war and revolution. In art, the passion for the real ended up erasing the boundaries between art and life by privileging event, performance, and presentation over representation. For instance, theater questioned the distinctions between spectacle and audience; the visual arts favored concrete forms over representational and abstract art (site-specific installations questioning the "neutral" space of the gallery, and participatory works challenging contemplative ones).

In many performances and real time events, the documentation of artworks often ended up exchanging places with the works themselves. Documentation usually made in a different medium from that of the "original work," went on to perform its own engagement with audiences and often through the mass media. Art's emphasis on real things and real structures, real gestures in real life, as a result, eventually transferred the question of representation to the realm of documentation (usually in the form of photography or video). And thus, photos and video documentary of performances and other fleeting artworks, while aiming to produce some permanence of that which was ephemeral, eventually became their double—representational images with a life and a media all their own. As mediators between the original works and audiences elsewhere, these images often circulated through books, in the news media, and the art market, as they became more than just records for archives. Examples come from performance, happenings, earth works, and participatory propositions, which, at the same time that they refused

---

[51]   Ibid, 32.

representation—opting instead to explore the "real" elements of art—in many cases, resulted in an other type of documentary representation of the real event. As art historian Miwon Kwon observed in reference to many 1960s happenings including the famous Yoko Ono *Cut Piece* performed at the Carnegie Hall, in New York, in 1965, for instance, many artworks and performances that were critical of the commodity status of art and produced the dematerialization of the art object in the late 1960s, ended up a decade later, having its scores, its relics, and its other various performance paraphernalia commodified by the art market and collected just the same, and even with the encouragement of the artists themselves.[52]

Before I examine in more detail this passage from the art object to participatory propositions in the 1960s—the dematerialization of art and the transformation of the role of the beholder in the unfolding of the artwork—in chapter four, dedicated to the legacies of Lygia Clark and Hélio Oiticica, I will explore the relationship between the real and representation in the work of media theorist Vilém Flusser, who connected many of the questions addressed in chapter two existentially and philosophically—from the Holocaust to the question of language, culture, and media arts, especially the relationship between the real, the abstract and the concrete in Brazilian art. And given that Flusser's books from the 1960s are published in Portuguese, and remain without translation, I will also dedicate some pages of the next chapter to analyzing them.

---

[52]   For a first analysis, manifestos, and other many primary documents of this period see: Lucy Lippard, *Six Years: The Dematerialization of the Art Object from 1966 to 1972* (Los Angeles: University of California Press, 1997).

Chapter 3

Vilém Flusser's Archive: a Topology of Translations Without Foundations

Of the thirty-two years this original and controversial philosopher lived in Brazil—from 1940 to 1972 when he left the country to lead a truly nomadic international life of lectures and publications—the 1960s marked the incorporation of Portuguese into his philosophical practice, as well as his activist engagement with the effervescent cultural context of the era. Vilém Flusser's (1920-1991) lifelong interest in the philosophy of language and communication is expressed throughout his writings and especially in his first three books, written in Portuguese, and published in São Paulo between 1963 and 1967.

Although Flusser became famous as a media philosopher in the 1980s, the focus of his thought was on dialogue and upon an analysis without foundations. This included speculation on language and science, theology and design, philosophy and history. Flusser's editor Andreas Ströl underlined the focus of his thought: "Flusser posits that existential 'uprooting' is a condition of freedom."[53] Lack of foundation for the philosopher was both an ethical existential condition and a philosophical perspective. Ströl further observed that, "Flusser divides European intellectuals into two camps. One person sees in him a pessimistic, cynical prognosticator of the decline of our writing-based culture and, with it, Western civilization, as we know it. Another sees in him the prophet of a new, posthistorical humanism that will rise up from the present environment of media and communication structures. Flusser

---

[53]   Andreas Ströl, "Introduction," in *Vilém Flusser Writings*, Andreas Ströhl, Ed., and Erik Eisel, Trans. (Minneapolis: University of Minesota Press, 2002), xvi.

himself encouraged both of these views."[54] And of course, these two views are not contradictory. The pessimist and the visionary are combined in writings that looked at the past from a perspective of the present and of the future.

Contrary to the popular Brazilian belief (and colonialist mindset) that one philosophizes better in German, French, or English, Flusser's multidimensional philosophy based on the fluidity of thought among multiple languages, states just the opposite. Without privileging any language as foundational, he found Portuguese—the language of his involuntary exile, for instance—to be non-contaminated by traditional metaphysical terminology, and thus capable of becoming a true language for philosophy in the future. Flusser wrote primarily in German, Portuguese, English, and French without privileging any of them. *Bodenlos*—meaning bottomless, lack of foundation—is the title of his philosophical autobiography written mostly in the mid 1970s after he left Brazil, finally published in Germany in 1992 after his tragic death in Prague in 1991.

Without Translation: Flusser's Brazilian Writings of the 1960s

Over the three-decades he lived in Brazil, and especially in the reflections he made about that period after he left that country, Flusser connected many threads between Brazilian and European history. His first three books— *Língua e Realidade* [Language and Reality], 1963; *A História do Diabo* [The History of the Devil], 1965; and *Da Religiosidade: A Literatura e o Senso de Realidade* [*Of Religiosity: Literature and the Sense of Reality*], 1967— were recently republished for the first time since the 1960s.[55] With the exception of *The*

---

54   Ibid., ix-x.

55   Recent editions of Flusser's books in Brazil include: *O Mundo Codificado: Por uma filosofia do design e da comunicação,*

History of the Devil, the other two remain without translation into other languages.[56] The major theme that traverses these three very different books is the idea that language produces reality. Throughout his life the philosopher worked on variations of this central theme, constantly translating, retranslating, and rewriting his essays in a process in which each new language enriched the meaning of the previous one. With each new translation of a text he wrote a new version of his ideas by weaving fresh connections and unforeseen conceptual possibilities.[57] Flusser's *Língua e Realidade* [Language and Reality] demonstrates this reasoning through a phenomenological thinking-in-translation, which includes the examination of partial translations, productive mistranslations, and misreadings, as well as the impossibility of the translation of certain words and structures from one language into another. Given that for this polyglot thinker language is always plural, instead of abstracting differences among Western languages, which one must do in order to translate, he probed these

---

Rafael Cardoso, org. (São Paulo: CosacNaify, 2007) [a compilation of design essays published between 1973 and 1991]; *Bodenlos: Uma Autobiografia Filosófica* (São Paulo: Annablume 2007) [originally published in 1992]; *A História do Diabo* (São Paulo: Annablume, 2005) [1965]; *Língua e Realidade* (São Paulo: Annablume, second edition 2004, third edition 2007) [1963]; *Da Religiosidade: A Literatura e o Senso de Realidade* (São Paulo: Escrituras, 2002) [1967]; and *Filosofia da Caixa Preta* (Rio de Janeiro: Relume Dumará, 2002) [1983].

[56]   *A História do Diabo* was also published in German as *Die Geschichte des Teufels*, Andreas Müller-Pohle, Ed. (Göttingen: European Photograph, 1993) and in Czech as *Pribeh d'ábla*, 1997.

[57]   Flusser's practice of translation as a creative process has been examined by Rainer Guldin, "Translation, Self-Translation, Retranslation: Exploring Vilém Flusser's Multilingual Writing Practice" in *Das Spiel mit der Übersetzung. Figuren der Mehrsprachigkeit im Werk Vilém Flussers*, Ranier Guldin, Ed. (Basel: Tübingen, 2004), 99-118.

differences while contrasting multiple worldviews, which languages produce and enable.

Language and Reality: Epistemological, Ethical, and Ontological Considerations

In *Língua e Realidade* [Language and Reality] Flusser used two diagrams to argue that many philosophical categories of Western knowledge are in fact structures of language—and thus dependent upon grammar, syntax, and semantic horizon, which vary, whether one is thinking in Greek, Latin, or German. To make this point he uses Portuguese as his instrument of investigation, and translates into it words, concepts, and structures from German, English, and Czech—while allowing readers to capture the dynamic changes in meaning among these languages. To Portuguese, which Flusser saw as a "language of digression," he brought a fresh, direct, and clear style that is anti-academic, yet scholarly; simultaneously communicative and speculative. In *Língua e Realidade* [Language and Reality] Flusser privileged Portuguese over other languages for its richness of meanings and plastic structure, as well as its lack of metaphysical foundation. In the book's preface Gustavo Bernardo Krause observed:

> We are dealing with a masterpiece, because it is the first book of this thinker and also because the book is absolutely original. Never before or after has the philosophy of language been discussed as in this work, based not only on erudite information but also upon the experience of an exiled polyglot. *Língua e Realidade* was written in Portuguese by a Czech philosopher who usually wrote in German. By writing this book Fluser felt he

incorporated Portuguese as a third mother language.[58]

Related to the notion that language produces reality is Flusser's emphasis on translation: "The problem of translation and translatability takes on the cosmic dimensions of all existential issues: it encompasses everything."[59] For him, the issue of translation was at once an epistemological problem—a question of knowing; an ethical problem—an issue of value; and a problem of meaning—an ontological dilemma. The question of language indeed traversed and shaped his philosophy and existence. From this perspective of language and communications he later reflected on media, on the development of technical images, and upon the future of Western civilization.

The History of the Devil: Theology, Evolution, and Teleology

Flusser's second book *A História do Diabo* [*The History of the Devil*] explored the issue of time. Published in 1965, it was in fact his first book written in German and then translated into Portuguese. With wit, humor, and a sense of reflective adventure, the book examined the idea of linear progress by combining science and theology, which, much opposed to common preconception, Flusser identified with the devil. History thus began theologically with man's fall from paradise, and historically with the invention of writing in Mesopotamia. According to Flusser, the realm of God, the divine and sacred dimension, is timeless and eternal, and our

---

[58]   Gustavo Bernardo Krause also mentions that Brazilian critic Anatol Rosenfeld, who wrote a review of *Língua e Realidade* in 1964 and despite disagreeing with Flusser's thesis recommended the book as a masterpiece of profound intuition, analytical power, and sharp insight.

[59]   *Vilém Flusser Writings*, 194.

earthly mundane world is temporal. Therefore, the book sees the devil as synonymous with history, with progress and evolution; and God is equated with the notion of infinite time and eternity. "The history of the devil is the history of progress. Our book should have been called 'Evolution' but the term would have caused some misunderstandings. Evolution as the history of progress is the history of the devil."[60] Flusser explored in this book the history of science, Buddhist philosophy and Judeo-Christian theology. The book chapters were structured after "the work of the devil," that is, according to the way the devil exercises his influence upon men through the seven capital sins, which Flusser further organized hierarchically and dynamically from lust to sloth, while reinterpreting them in the following positive light:

> Pride is self-conciousness. Greed is economy. Lust is instinct (and the affirmation of life). Gluttony is the improvement of living standards. Envy is the fight for social justice and political freedom. Wrath is the refusal to accept the limitations imposed on human will; and therefore it is dignity. Sloth or Sadness is the stage reached by calm philosophical meditation.[61]

---

[60]   Vilém Flusser, *A História do Diabo* (São Paulo: Annablume, 2005), 24. Translation mine.

[61]   Ibid., 25. Contrasting with the contemporary emphasis on speed and multitasking, philosophers such as Kierkegaard, artists such as Hélio Oiticica, and cultural critics such as Oscar Wilde have also praised sloth as an essential condition for philosophical and creative practices. More recently, media archeologist Siegfried Zielinski has argued for a cool down period of media reflection in the twenty-first century.

The History of the Devil also identified history with the invention of the alphabet and of writing (made popular after a few millennia through the invention of typography). To this definition of history Flusser later added a third major technological revolution—the invention of photography and thus of the making of technical images—that according to him would lead to the end of history and to the beginning of a posthistorical era. In his 1960s writings, however, Flusser examined the moment of crisis of Modern history while pointing out that a future epoch was not yet born. It was only in the 1970s, and especially after he returned to Europe, that he would theorize the shift from industrial to information-digital culture, and thus the passage from history to posthistory. Marking this transition was his most famous book *Für eine Philosophie der Fotografie* [*Towards a Philosophy of Photography*] first published in Germany in 1983, distinguishing him as an original media theoretician who advanced and urged an equally radical new Philosophy. Flusser's enthusiasm for cybernetics and digital technologies acquires a different dimension when positioned in the context of his earlier writings on language, history and religion; it is also important to understand his embrace of the Brazilian utopian project, followed in the late 1960s by an even more radical embrace of exile.

Of Religiosity: Literature and the Sense of Reality (Dimensions of the Sacred and the Poetic)

Flusser's third book *Da Religiosidade: A Literatura e o Senso de Realidade* [*Of Religiosity: Literature and the Sense of Reality,* 1967] contrasts with his first two books by being a compilation of short essays that more urgently addressed the 1960s zeitgeist. His preference for the essay form, according to the philosopher, affected not only the form of his writing (such as a short text without footnotes) but also the content, not to mention the way the author engages and reaches audiences. He contrasted the essay to academic writing: "Academic style is a special kind of style. It unites intellectual honesty with existential dishonesty, because the person who has recourse to it commits the intellect and withdraws the body."[62] I believe that an additional reason for Flusser's preference for the essay might have been his desire to write for newspapers. In Brazil of the 1950s and 1960s, important cultural discussions took place in literary and cultural supplements of the most important periodicals of São Paulo and Rio de Janeiro. Flusser wanted to engage in this conversation, and most essays in his book were originally published in the newspaper *O Estado de São Paulo*. While these essays highly praised current art and poetry movements, they were often critical of their shortcomings. Furthermore, the book title— *Da Religiosidade* —calls attention to our continuous loss of the sense of the sacred, as well as the superficiality and the conformity of thought in contemporary life. The choice of articles for the book were made, according to the philosopher, following vaguely thematic criteria:

> Literature, whether philosophical or not, is the place in which the sense of reality is articulated. And 'sense of reality' is, under certain aspects, a synonym of religiosity. Real is everything in which we believe. During the pre-Christian era the real was nature, and the pre-Christian religions believed in the forces of nature, which they made divine. During the Middle Ages the real was transcendent, as is the God of Christianity. But beginning in the XV century the real is problematized. Nature is questioned and put in doubt, and the faith on

---

[62]   Ibid., 117.

a transcendent reality loses ground. Thus our
situation is characterized by an unreal
sensation and by the search for a new sense of
religiosity. This is the theme of these chosen
essays.[63]

Central to the book are two philosophical essays—
"Pensamento e Reflexão" [Thought and Reflection] and "Da
Dúvida" [Of Doubt]—that contextualize the loss of the sacred as
that dimension which is unknowable. They were not written for
newspapers but for more specialized publications.[64] Flusser's
intuition was that there is something fundamentally wrong and
insufficient with the Cartesian rationality and the pure
materialism of science and technology. For the philosopher there
was always something more than material reality, which poetry
touches and articulates as the limit of thought: "Poetry produces
language because it articulates the inarticulate." [...] The
inarticulate is inexhaustible."[65] These philosophical essays are
critical of the limitations of the Enlightenment's
instrumentalization of reason, to which Flusser opposed the
reflective nature of philosophy, the inventive nature of literature,
and the sense of wonder of religious affect. According to
Flusser's introduction to the book, the Modern era religiosity
ended up in the total and boring profanation that is technology.
And he urged that a new era bring about new religious
possibilities:

---

[63]   Flusser, *Da Religiosidade*, 13. Translation mine.

[64]   They were published in the *Revista Brasileira de Filosofia*
and the *Revista do Instituto Tecnológico da Aeronáutica, Dept. de
Humanidades*, respectively.

[65]   Flusser, *Da Religiosidade*, 57.

Indeed, all of our creative activities,
including scientific and artistic ones are
dedicated to the effort to create a new field
open to religiosity. With our intellect we
are still modern, but with our religiosity we
already participate in the era to come.
Which is the same as saying that we are
beings in transition and in search of the
future. And if the traditional religions are
unacceptable, and the exotic religions are
exposed as escapist, and if the detour of
religion towards politics, economy, and
technology disappoints, we remain with
our religious hunger unsatisfied.[66]

In a recent passage about Flusser that could have been a
review of his third book, cultural critic Sean Cubitt emphasized
the European Gnostic tradition present in Flusser's thinking:

It is sad therefore to note that materialism
has often—though not universally—
eschewed any address to the sacred. By this
I do not mean that materialism in any way
fails for lack of a theology, nor that the
sacred forms some ontological ground on
which the material world is more deeply
founded. Rather, what has been often
lacking is a commitment to understanding
that affect which we recognize under the
rubric of sacredness, an elevation beyond
not merely the instinctual but also the
intellectual pleasures, a yearning apart from

---

[66]   Ibid., 20-21.

the desire for justice, peace and plenty for
all.[67]

The religiosity Flusser envisioned for the era to come
would be articulated in the 1970s and 1980s by his media theory.
His hopes for a telematic culture and discussions of humanism
and posthistory all contributed to the renovation of the sense of
wonder which he connected with the sacred, and which this
book *Da Religiosidade* [*Of Religiosity*] so poignantly
emphasized.

The Brazil Project: Utopia, Revolution, and the Notion of Homeland[68]

Flusser's first three books reflect his engagement with
the utopian Brazil project. During the 1950s and 1960s he was at
the same time a critic and an enthusiastic articulator of the new
Brazil under construction: he connected Prague and São Paulo;
European and South American modernisms; Kafka, Guimarães
Rosas and the São Paulo Concrete poets.[69]

---

[67]   Sean Cubitt's review of the book *Deep Time of the Media: Toward an Archaeology of Hearing and Seeing by Technical Means* by Siegfried Zielinski, in *Leonardo Reviews*, August 2007, http://www.leonardo.info/reviews/aug2007/deep_cubitt.html

[68]   For further discussion of these relations in Brazilian modern and contemporary art please see my essay: "Tropical Modern: The Political Ambivalence of Cultural Remix," in *Canal Contemporâneo*, December 2006. http://www.canalcontemporaneo.art.br/documenta 12magazines/archives/001001.php

[69]   About Flusser's relation to these writers, see Gustavo Bernardo Krause, "Da Prece à Literatura," in *Vilém Flusser no Brasil*, Gustavo Bernardo Krause and Ricardo Mendes, Org. (Rio de Janeiro: Relume Dumará, 2000). The radical verbal and visual innovations of Brazil in the 1950s were an intrinsic part of the developmental years that characterized President Jucelino Kubitschek's government (1956-1960): the building of a democratic society based on a modern national

Flusser sought integration into Brazilian life as long as he believed a new type of civilization was possible from its complex mixture. He explained: "For decades, I was involved in an experiment to synthesize Brazilian culture from a larger mix of Western European, Eastern European, African, East Asian, and Indian cultural phenomena."[70] In later essays in which he reflected upon the Brazilian project, such as the 1981 "Mythical, Historical, and Posthistorical Existence" he begins by stating: "The Brazilian situation is extraordinarily instructive for Europeans."[71] Flusser observed that the different Western developmental epochs—mythic-magical; historical (equated with writing, linear time, and later with logical reason); and post-historical (equated with telematics and digital images)—are layers which in Europe tend to be stacked upon each other while in Brazil coexisted side by side. At first, he considered this coexistence of different temporalities to be part of Brazil's open possibilities. However, after the military coup in 1964, and a decade of a repressive and nationalist technocratic government, he realized that the lack of communication among the different social classes and cultures was a problematic structure headed for disaster.[72]

---

industry; the construction of the new capital—Brasília, a monument to the International Style; all accompanied by an unprecedented cultural effervescence that justified the country's leap into the future (fifty years in five was the motto of President Kubitschek) shaking up most forms of artistic expression throughout the late 1960s including music, architecture, theater, poetry, literature, visual arts, cinema, and design.

[70]   *Vilém Flusser Writings*, 91.

[71]   Ibid., 117.

[72]   The year 1968 marked the beginning of an era of state terrorism in Brazil. On December 13th the military government issued the AI-5 (Fifth Institutional Act) signed by military President General Costa e Silva. The AI-5 closed Congress and suspended all political and constitutional rights, opening the way to political persecution, torture, and censorship. Following the interruption by a military coup in 1964,

In *Bodenlos: a Philosophical Autobiography* Flusser described the men and women he met in São Paulo and who shaped his intellect. They are a total of eleven—nine men and two women—seven were born in Brazil and four were immigrants like him. And despite the importance of these relationships, or perhaps because of them, after he lost the belief that Brazil, at the edge of Western culture, could become a promising model for the future of Western civilization, Flusser opted to live in permanent exile and become a foreigner to every culture:

> When I arrived in Brazil and as soon as I managed to free myself from the gas chambers to a certain extent, I was carried away by this fever. I indulged myself into building a new, humane home free of prejudice. It was not until the *golpe*, the army's coup d'état, that I became more humble. But not because I understood the Brazilian coup to be a reactionary intervention—the way most European observers interpreted it—but because I recognized it as the first manifestation of a Brazilian homeland.[73]

---

presidential elections were not held again until 1989. Ironically, during the country's darkest era of political oppression in 1970, Brazil was the first country in history to win the World Cup for the third time. The soccer world leadership produced the strongest display of patriotic fever. It was somehow the certainty that the "sleeping giant" had finally been awakened. The nation wrapped itself in the colors of the flag and repeated the World cup theme song as a mantra for years to come.

[73]   *Vilém Flusser Writings*, 97.

Believing that "patriotism is the symptom of an aesthetic disease," in 1972, Flusser left Brazil and returned to Europe.

The violence of history and the ethics of exile

The decision to embrace exile in a more radical way strengthened the ethical and existential choices that guided Flusser's philosophy. His decision to "take up residency in homelessness" reinforced his desire to free himself from any attachment to a homeland. He understood this attachment as the root of preconceptions and unquestioned values: "The loss of home sheds light on this secret. [...] It discloses what it really is: the seat of most (perhaps all) of our prejudices—the judgments made before any conscious judgments."[74] And he further connects this familiar attachment to a homeland as the root of false aesthetic values: "The immigrant becomes even more unsettling to the native, uncannier than the traveler out there, because he reveals the banality of the sacred to the native. He is hateful; he is ugly, because he exposes the beauty of home as nothing more than pretty kitsch."[75] Flusser saw this aesthetic handicap as the root of ethnocentrism, which could escalate into nationalism, fascism, and ethnic pogroms. That is why for him the Zionist project was never appealing. His multicultural upbringing and multiple exiles allowed him to see how signs are naturalized and made transparent and thus invisible.

At first he struggled with the devastating sense of loss brought about by the holocaust in which all his family and friends were killed: "All of the people to whom I was mysteriously bound in Prague were murdered. All of them. The

---

[74]   Ibid., 93.

[75]   Ibid., 95.

Jews in gas chambers, the Czechs in the Resistance, the Germans on the Russian front."[76] But he later found an incredible sense of freedom from no longer having any ties to a country. He reflected upon this condition of exile in various essays and spent his life transforming a negative experience as an expellee into a positive creative force by proposing:

> We, the uncounted millions of emigrants (whether we are guest workers, expellees, or intellectuals traveling from one seminar to another), do not recognize ourselves as outsiders, but rather as pioneers of the future. For this reason, the Vietnamese in California, the Turks in Germany, the Palestinians in the Persian Gulf, and the Russian scientists at Harvard should not be considered pitiful victims in need of aid. One should not aid so that they can go back to their homelands. Instead, they should be considered role models whose examples we follow in case we are sufficiently daring. Certainly, only the expelled and emigrants can allow themselves such thoughts, not the expellers or those who stayed behind; for emigration is a creative activity, but it also entails suffering[77]

The theme of exile in his philosophy connects an existential ethics with a visionary enthusiasm for telematics, thus allowing us to relate the idea of rootlessness with a media philosophy that theorized the non-linear logic of networked technology. Furthermore, his philosophy always sought the

---

[76]   Ibid., 94.

[77]   Ibid., 92.

dialogue with other disciplines whether literature, sciences, art, logic, theology, music, or design. His ability to make comparisons among different elements and dimensions as he does for instance in the first chapter of the book *Da Religiosidade* [*Of Religiosity*], making a parallel between music and religion, characterized his elastic thinking and it is in this sense that he should be understood as a "media philosopher." Siegfried Zielinsky's insightful archeology of hearing and seeing by technical means places Flusser among the most original thinkers. Zielinsky points out how Flusser's presence in the media debates of the 1980s was important for new media artists who wanted to change the world and saw no connection between their ideas and the more abstract Lacanian and poststructuralist theories, and thus were thirsty for new impulses:

> In his lectures, Flusser often jumped back and forth between the reality of facticity and fecund speculation, or sketched the identity of thought that operates within the strong tension of *curiositas* and *necessitas* (curiosity and necessity) as [Giovan Battista Della] Porta defined the two most important motivations for the work of the researcher. Flusser charismatically embodied this identity. [...] For established academe, his thinking, characterized by its mental leaps between the disciplines, is unacceptable even today. [78]

Flusser's analysis of words and images exemplifies this type of articulation as he contrasted the one-dimensional verbal

---

[78]   Siegfried Zielinski, *Deep Time of the Media: Toward an Archaeology of Hearing and Seeing by Technical Means* (Cambridge, MA: MIT Press, 2006), 97.

linear structure of one-word-after-another with the two-dimensional plane of photographic images, and further with the zero dimension of computational visualization. Always seeking to expand dialogue, Flusser bridged many worlds and found original correspondences and analogies among different elements. He called attention, for instance, to the fuzzy passage among the three orders of magnitude in science: the Newtonian world of centimeters and seconds; a second bigger order of magnitude measurable in light-years, in which Einsteinian rules apply; and a third micro world of nanoseconds, in which the rules of quantum mechanics are valid. "In each of these worlds, we have to think differently, try to imagine differently, and act differently."[79] And that is what he continuously did.

Flusser argued, for instance, that linear writing produced causal explanations and logical thought processes to which numerical codes have been attached throughout the entire history of the West. "Recently, the numeric code broke out of the alphabetical code, freed itself from the pressure of linearity, and switched over from numeric to digital."[80] And of course this realization has important consequences to image making and reception. According to him, images are no longer two-dimensional translations of a four-dimensional world. They are two-dimensional planes created from zero-dimensional elements. Synthetic images are calculations, pure abstractions, "pure aesthetics." Thus he concluded that digital images were no longer ontologically and epistemologically suspicious of simulacra, as they once were for Plato and for a theological iconoclastic tradition inspired by Judaism. They rather *leap* from a linear logic into the zero-dimension of computations. They are a conceptual leap of imagination.

---

[79]   *Vilém Flusser Writings*, 89.

[80]   Ibid., 113.

As media art histories abandon the rhetoric of "the new" for a historiography that does not simply "sweep up the pieces into a sensible heap,"[81] Flusser's fluidity, range, and elasticity of thought constitute a high standard for a more rigorous yet accessible engagement with philosophy and history. His philosophizing-in-translation combined with a phenomenologist capacity to capture the sacred and the poetic dimensions of the world, aside from his ethical position of exile and lack of foundation as a condition of freedom, are a fecund source of inspiration for media histories to come. Our task is to continue writing histories with this kind of insight.

Flusser's Concept of Techno-imagination

Vilém Flusser became internationally known as a media philosopher with the publication of *Für eine Philosophie der Fotografie*, 1983, and throughout that decade he developed and promoted a theory of images based on the concept of techno-imagination. In a recent essay that examined the concept, Flusser scholar Rainer Guldin argued that Flusser's notion of techno-imagination circumvents the Western philosophical iconoclastic bias, as well as Flusser's own.[82] Flusser's notion

---

[81]   "Introduction" Michael Punt, *Leonardo Electronic Almanac*, Volume   15,   Number 9   -   10,   2007. <http://leoalmanac.org/>http://leoalmanac.org

[82]   Rainer Guldin, "Iconoclasm and Beyond: Vilém Flusser Concept of Techno-Imagination," *Journal of the Swiss Association of Communication and Media Research*, Vol. 7, N. 2, 2007, pp. 63-83. In this essay, Guldin refers to the examples given by Arlindo Machado in *O Quarto Iconoclasmo* [The Fourth Iconoclasm] to list four iconoclastic moments that privileged words as critical of images distortion/illusion in Western though: first, Plato's *Republic* and Judeo-Christian-Muslim book-based theology; second, the image wars of the Byzantine Empire between the 8th and 9th centuries A.D.; third, Calvin's Protestant Reformation; and fourth, the vein of contemporary theory that includes Guy Debord, Frederic Jameson, and Jean Baudrillard. Guldin's

begins with the dichotomy between the visual and the verbal languages as they reflect upon life experiences as well as upon each other, in turn producing images of a different kind. He traced this dialectic to different historical epochs as follows:

> First, man took a step back from his life-world, to imagine it. Then, man stepped back from the imagination, to describe it. Then, man took a step back from the linear, written critique, to analyze it. And finally, owing to a new imagination, man projected synthetic images out of analysis. Certainly, this series of gestures should not be considered a linear sequence of events.[83]

Although these periods seem to constitute a dialectical progression, Flusser states that these events are not to be considered linear, given that individual gestures neither replace each other nor cancel each other out, but instead overlap and mesh together. Nevertheless, Guldin poignantly observed that Flusser's view of traditional images is a weak point in his "picture theory" because he did not differentiate historically among different types of images and simply refers to images and texts as a binary opposition.[84] Thus, at the same time that Flusser identifies the innovative and generative potential of technical images, he simplifies the prior traditional relations between words and images, therefore ignoring the textual dimension of

---

discussion of Flusser's concept of techno-imagination is based on two Flusser articles written in German: *In Umbrich der menschlichen Beziehungen?* (1996) and *Für eine Theorie de Technoimagination* (1998), as well as in the *Towards a Philosophy of Photography* (1983).

[83]   Vilém Flusser, "A New Imagination," in *Vilém Flusser Writings*, 110-116.

[84]   Rainer Guldin, "Iconoclasm and Beyond," 69.

pictures (the relations between painting and poetry, for instance, in the tradition of *Ut Pictura Theoria*), and the visual/pictorial dimension of texts (such as graphic-spatial dimensions and in Ekphrasis descriptions of the visual).[85] In addition, there are other intimate and complex relations between words and images, such as the ancient "art of memory," in which images have served as an architectural frame, as mnemonic devices that aided poets and public performers with a system of storage/retrieval of large amounts of information needed in speeches that could not rely on written texts.[86]

In his essay "A New Imagination" Flusser argues that traditional images were a step back from the four-dimensional world in the direction of two-dimensional abstraction, while technical images were the result of a gesture that moves forward, from the zero conceptual dimension of calculations and numerical operations to the concrete images of visualized information—a second degree of abstraction, a radical and concrete imagination diametrically opposed to the traditional images and classical forms of mimetic imagination. For this concreteness (opposed to the notion that abstractions made after mimetic representations are illusions, a false copy, or at least a lower dimensional reality), Flusser emphasized the generative, programmable potential of technology that made possible the visualization of information as a product of pure calculations. And the example he gave of techno-imagination was the use of images in the sciences, such as photographs of cosmic events, which are only properly understood by astronomers. Thus for the

---

[85]   For such interconnections between images, text, and power, see W.T.J. Mitchell *Picture Theory* (Chicago: The University of Chicago Press, 1994). Also connecting images and words, image traces and language traces, are Derrida's *Truth in Painting*, and *Memoirs of the Blind*.

[86]   Francis Yates, *The Art of Memory* (Chicago: University of Chicago Press, 2001).

media philosopher, digital images are concrete, and therefore ontologically and epistemologically different from the abstracting process of traditional images, which were based on mimetic representation and therefore were traces of retroactive memory.

In his introduction to *Iconoclash*—an ambitious and comprehensive anthology about the image wars, from East and West and from the Middle Ages to Modernism in Science, Religion, and Art—Bruno Latour's observations about scientific images can, I believe, illustrate Flusser's concept of techno-imagination. Latour observes that "isolated, a scientific image has no referent [...] a table of figures will lead to a grid that will lead to a photograph that will lead to a diagram that will lead to a paragraph that will lead to a statement. The whole series has meaning but none of its elements has any sense."[87] Latour also compares the invisibility of the image referent in science and religion. In science, for instance, "if you wanted to abandon the image and turn your eyes instead to the prototype *that* they are supposed to figure out, you would see less, infinitely less. You would be blind for good." Scientific images, as both Flusser and Latour pointed out, enable the visualization of concepts, data, and models of the physical world, which are invisible to the eye. Made by different means and with different functions, how do these images contrast and compare with our understanding of visual representation in general?

---

[87]   Bruno Latour, "What is Iconoclash? Or Is There A World Beyond the Image Wars?" in *Iconoclash: Beyond the Image Wars in Science, Religion, and Art*, Bruno Latour and Peter Weibel, eds. (Karlsruhe: ZKM center for Art and Media and Cambridge, Mass: MIT Press, 2002), 34.

Forging A Second-degree Criticism

Flusser's concept of techno-imagination advances a new form of image criticism beyond traditional criticism, which according to him consisted in explaining the relationship between pictures and the objects they represented by translating connotative elements into denotative meanings. For the philosopher, these explanations were not radical enough because they were dependent upon the logic of linear writing. Therefore, he argued that a second-degree criticism was needed as a critique of traditional image criticism itself. "This new form of critique implies a radically new form of imagination, diametrically opposed to the old one, and a new use of imagery, ensuing from a calculating, computational gesture."[88] We may ask at this point what this second-degree critique really is, how does it challenge other types of image analysis, and who might be performing it today? Will it be performed by fast-forwarding and/or rewinding? By interdisciplinary breadth or analytical depth?

Contemporary artist Paul Miller, aka DJ Spooky, describes the 21st century mediascape in terms of code and increasing speed, while stating that the questions it poses have no answer:

> With our cell phones able to beam us high resolution videos, our podcast attention span searches for the next download [...] our billboards switch images with blinding speed, our advertisement drenched urban landscape that stretches from the city to the suburbs, and the exurbs beyond. These hyper-accelerated phenomena of what I like to call 'prosthetic-

---

[88]   Rainer Guldin, "Iconoclasm and Beyond," 79.

realism' are the principle metaphors for a
culture that has shifted away from the physical
objects of the 20th century, to the wireless
imagination of the 21st. Today, our
contemporary information ecology is a coded
landscape: it is a Sphinx that asks a riddle for
which there is no answer—how do you make
sense of the datacloud? [89]

For Miller, the remix is capable of absorbing all of this
eclectic acceleration of information. Yet, how does it contribute
to forge or to undermine media theories? If, as Miller also
observed elsewhere in this article, "the method of the inquiry is
what drives the investigation," then with which methodology do
we examine the new wireless imagination? And what happens if
the investigation in turn subverts the methodology that is driving
it? How would Flusser's second-degree criticism, for instance,
avoid the power of illusion, seduction and persuasion of
traditional images, which iconoclasts insist have led in the past
to idolatry and irrational behavior?

In an article from 1991, titled "Media Aesthetics in
Europe" Wolfgang Schirmacher examined what he saw as a
general European bias towards contemporary technology,
arguing that media criticism needs to be based on media
experience: "Media aesthetics has to be attuned to the global
changes in technology."[90] Elsewhere, Schirmacher's concept of
Homo Generator affirms that, "a philosopher worthy of his or
her profession has to love and hate technology at the same time,

---

[89]   Paul Miller "Film Form/Film Formlessness" distributed at his
seminar at the European Graduate School in June 2005.

[90]   Wolfgang Schirmacher, "Media Aesthetics in Europe." Paper
delivered at the conference *The Media in Europe*, Paris, 1983.
Published   on   the   web:
http://www.egs.edu/faculty/schirmacher/aesth.html

acknowledging our debt to Kierkegaard who made such contradictory moves a powerful indirect communication."[91] Such emphasis on the benefits of contradictory approaches is also the organizing concept of Bruno Latour and Peter Weibel's *Iconoclash*. As the title of the book suggests, we are between two contradictory urges: one iconophile and the other iconoclastic, and both are uncertain about how images represent, control, communicate and seduce us.

However, from Flusser's point of view, a techno-imagination was beyond this contradictory experience by being critical of the historiography that examined traditional images. Therefore, we may ask if Flusser's second-degree criticism—a new way of thinking about images based on a techo-imagination—must be born out of technological practices? Why couldn't it be born out of visual knowledge? After all, since the beginning of time, images have always and already been generative in the hands of designers, architects, and artists who project new products, spaces, and forms, by relating subject matter, concepts, form, and materials. Isn't visualization through working models of the world the way we always developed knowledge, exercised control, as well as created forms of entertainment?[92] How is then, new media art radically altering the way we think, visualize, store and analyze information, organize archives and write history? Can the changing relations between text-based knowledge, image-based knowledge, and body-based knowledge, which new media recombine, automatically produce the second-degree criticism Flusser

---

[91]   Wolfgang Schirmacher, "Homo Generator: Militant Media & Postmodern   Technology",   on   the   Web: http://www.egs.edu/faculty/schirmacher/homo.html

[92]   Are new efforts such as the book *Media Art Histories*, Oliver Grau, ed., MIT Press 2007, actually producing new methodology and insight? Can this expansion of media arts historiography fulfill Flusser's expectation of a techno-imagination second-degree criticism?

envisioned? Can the *remix* be both a creative practice and a
critical theory? Can the visual arts, sci-fi literature and film
today be more insightful than critical theory for understanding
contemporary culture?

Flusser's image theory not only celebrates the concrete
gesture of technical images but also the relational, inter-
subjective potential of digital communication technology, which
in chapter four, I argue, is not necessarily a product of new
media interactivity but of conceptual developments within
contemporary art. Flusser's emphasis upon new media
communication stressed the connections they enabled among
people and the expression of multiple points of view. We may
ask if cell phones and the Internet are fulfilling his dream of
communication, group collaboration and networking, by
bringing together today up to hundreds of thousands of
participants in domains such as Wikipedia, Second Life, and
Facebook? Is the explosion of videos on YouTube and Blogs
really increasing communication and collaboration?

Flusser's championing of new media in the 1980s
envisioned a more egalitarian and utopian future world based
upon telecommunication technology. His media theory carried
the cultural activism he shared with other thinkers in Brazil of
the 1950s, such as the modernist emphasis on concrete art as a
new language, capable of building reality. The iconoclastic, anti-
representational vein of modernism embraced by Brazilian
avant-gardes in the 1950s, which later also characterized
Flusser's concept of techno-imagination in the 1970s, confirms
what Alain Badiou identified as the twentieth century "passion
for the real"[93] the desire to affect change directly in life through
both art and politics.

---

[93]   Alain Badiou, *The Century*. Cambridge, UK: Polity Press,
2007.

Techno-Imagination and Concrete Art

When in the 1950s, Brazilian poets and artists tried to create a revolutionary new culture, they relied upon Concrete Art as a way beyond the illusionist devices of traditional mimetic representation. Perhaps because Brazilian culture was considered by many a second-hand copy of European and increasingly of U.S. cultures, artists and writers felt the need for radical inventions beginning from a *tabula rasa*, just like before them other modernist avant-gardes from less industrialized nations— such as the Italian Futurists and the Russian Constructivists—enthusiastically embraced technology as the answer, as the modern sensibility that would give birth to a new society.

In Brazil of the 1950s, concrete artists and poets also envisioned a new culture that would enlist the arts alongside city planning, industrialization, and new educational pedagogies as agents for social change. Flusser was then a cultural critic who participated in the public discussions by publishing his essays in São Paulo newspapers. In the essay titled "Concreto—Abstrato" he examined the project of Concrete poetry by stating "the creation of reality is a linguistic activity […] that by creating language, one is creating reality, thus the 'concrete.'"[94] He pointed out that the concrete São Paulo poets and their manifesto *The Plano-piloto Para Poesia Concreta* were visionary, however, still timid, both in theory and practice. And in the spirit of constructive criticism, he pointed out that these poets "discovered a new continent but they lack the courage to colonize it."[95] And Flusser concluded the article by saying that

---

[94]   Flusser, "Concreto-Abstrato," *Da Religiosidade: A Literatura e o Senso de Realidade*, 149-150. Translation mine.

[95]   Ibid. I find surprising the language Flusser used here in suggesting that the new discovered territory had to be *colonized*. After

"All of us, Westerners in general, and Brazilians in particular, are invested in the search for a new sense of reality. In this search, the Concrete poets form a vanguard, not necessarily the only one, nor the most successful, but certainly one of the more exciting."[96] The Brazilian Concrete movements of the 1950's in the visual arts developed in two separate veins: in São Paulo through the leadership of Waldemar Cordeiro they generated, among other expressions, Cordeiros' *Popcreto* assemblages leading to his pioneering late 1960s exploration of digital images,[97] while in Rio de Janeiro they led to the emphasis on experience in the Neoconcrete movement of 1959, and with the introduction of real time into space, the emphasis on experience produced audience participation in the works of among others, Lygia Clark and Hélio Oiticica examined in chapter 4.

In his autobiography, *Bodenlos*, Flusser states that one of the important and formative intellectual dialogues of his life was with the Swiss-born, São Paulo based artist Mira Schendel. Although visual arts were not very prominent up to that point in his scholarship, when Flusser left Brazil in 1972 for various personal, political, and professional reasons, he was involved in, among other projects, the curatorial organization of the segment "Art and Communication" for the *XII Bienal Internacional de São Paulo*, 1973. Flusser's curatorial project was not completely

---

all, Brazil's attempt in the 1950s was to leap fifty years in five to overcome its own colonialist past.

[96]   Ibid, 153. The "plano-piloto para poesia concreta" was the title of the concrete poetry manifesto published in the *antologia noigandres 5* and signed by Augusto de Campos, Décio Pignatari and Haroldo de Campos. "Plano-piloto" meaning pilot-plan is a reference to the city plan of Brasília, projected by Lucio Costa.

[97]   Giorgio Moscatti, "Waldemar Cordeiro Computer Art," first published as "Arte e Computação: Um Depoimento," in Cadernos MAC-2,   São   Paulo   (July   1986):   3-17. http://leonardo.info/isast/spec.projects/moscati.html

successful, in part due to lack of support from the bienal administration. It's promotion of public participation was a central issue, which ironically, after more than three decades, is being revisited as the center of the discussions of the upcoming São Paulo Bienal of 2008. Flusser scholar and biographer Ricardo Mendes from São Paulo pointed out the need for further research of his production from the early 1970s, so the link between Flusser's Brazilian and European periods can be better understood.[98]

---

[98]   Ricardo Mendes, "Rumo ao exílio: Vilém Flusser, 1972." Published on the author's web site only: http://www.fotoplus.com/rico/rmbiocv.htm

The Future of Flusser's Archive

Figure 9. Flusser archive Universität der Künste, Berlin, Germany. (Photo: Stephen Sinsley)

Figure 10. Vilém Flusser's traveling library is a central part of his archive, Universität der Künste, Berlin, Germany. (Photo: Stephen Sinsley)

Flusser's archive, first housed at the Academy of Media Arts in Cologne, Germany, has been located, since 2007, at the Universität der Künste in Berlin, Germany [*Figs. 9, 10*].[99] Directed by media theorist Siegfried Zielinski,[100] the archive contains Flusser's traveling library, copies of most of his publications and manuscripts, as well as correspondences, video and audiotapes, photographs and a few objects, including Flusser's computer.

Given Flusser's practice of translating his own essays and books by rewriting while simultaneously adding new meanings suggested by the language into which he transposed his thoughts, his publications are organized according to the four languages he wrote in—German, Portuguese, English and French—as well as according to a list of key terms that helps locate conceptually related essays within his inter-textual web.

---

[99]   http://flusser.khm.de is the official site of the Flusser Archive.

[100]   Siegfried Zielinski's approach to archives, as well as to media theory and archeology is critical of the current historiography of media. He insists upon the importance of approaching archives and media as particular and singular historical developments. See his *Deep Time of the Media: Towards an Archeology of Hearing and Seeing by Technical Means* (Cambridge, MA: MIT Press, 2006). Zielinski points out: "The generalization inherent in the term media is an invention of the twentieth century. Yet the various techniques for communicating, envisioning/visualizing, generating knowledge, and entertaining are considerably older. To circumvent the trap of historicization, they should not all be subsumed under the general heading of media. As artifacts that exist as constructs or only as blueprints and proposals they are particular, and as such they resist generalization. Researching and exploring these artifacts in detail and in a wider historical context demands a different approach than that of the established historiography of the media." Keynote lecture titled, "On Deep Time Relations Between Arts, Sciences and Technologies: Questioning the Established Concepts of Media," in the catalogue of *re:place 2007, The Second International Conference on the Histories of Media, Mart, Science and Technology*, Berlin, Germany, November 15-18, 2007, 78.

The topological nature of his archive challenges researchers to understand its nodal structure and connect the multiple points of Flusser's thought and life—which almost form a dynamic artistic project by itself.

Flusser's nomadic life had three anchor cities, not including multiple others in between: Prague in the Czech Republic, São Paulo in Brazil, and Robion in France. Since his death in 1991, there has been a yearly Flusser symposium in Prague with papers and lectures presented in Czech, German and English. Growing out of these international conferences was the publication in 2005, of *Flusser Studies*, an international, multilingual e-journal for cultural and media theory dedicated to the development of Flusser's thought with a wealth of links to existing sites and web resources.[101]

Because of the way Flusser connected multiple subjects and languages, most Flusser researchers can't know all of his work. Thus, to a certain extent, his archive urges collaborations, such as the book *Vilém Flusser: Uma Introdução* written by three Flusser scholars living in separate continents.[102] At the same time, however, based upon discussions that I observed (for instance, at the *re:place* conference in Berlin in 2007), there are Flusser scholars who try to re-territorialize him and argue

---

[101] *Flusserstudies.net* was created in 2005 by the Swiss Rainer Gulding and the German-American Anke Finger. It publishes two issues per year with essays in five languages, English, German, Portuguese, French and Czech. I was invited to organize issue 08 published in May of 2009, focusing on Flusser and art.

[102] For instance, there is a new introduction to Flusser written and translated by three *Flusser Studies* editors—Rainer Guldin responsible for the version in German, Anke Finger, who did the English translation, and Gustavo Bernardo, responsible for the Portuguese version. They each wrote their contribution in a different language and translated each other's essays. The Brazilian version came out first: Gustavo Bernardo, Anke Finger and Rainer Guldin, *Vilém Flusser Uma Introdução*, (São Paulo: Annablume, 2008). The German and English versions are under production.

passionately, from different cultural perspectives—European or South American—about "their" different Flusser. The fluidity of Flusser's own transdisciplinary thinking, polyglot practice, and nomadic life makes his archive a topology of philosophical and media communication performances—a mixture of scholarly, critical, and creative practices that included collaborations with artists, such as the French conceptual artist and video maker Fred Forest, as well as at least one ambitious and complex curatorial project, which Flusser developed for the São Paulo Bienal of 1973.[103]

Despite the growing international interest in Flusser and the constant new research being done on his work, for example about the relationship between Flusser and other media theorists such as Marshall McLuhan, the structure of his archive, as such, also offers ground for future research.

---

[103] Ricardo Mendes, "Bienal de São Paulo 1973 – Flusser como curador: uma experiência inconclusa," paper presented at the Coloquium *A terceira margem: Vilém Flusser e o Brasil*, Germersheim, Germany, 10.2006. Available on the author's website: http://www.fotoplus.com/flusser/

Chapter 4

Lygia Clark and Hélio Oiticica: Legacies and Archives of Participatory Art

This chapter discusses the artistic legacies of Brazilian artists Lygia Clark (1920-1988) and Hélio Oiticica (1937-1980), focusing on the interactive vocabularies developed from their participatory creations of the 1960s and 1970s and pointing to the practical and conceptual relevance of these vocabularies for the changing ontology of the archive. The chapter also explores the critical and original way Clark and Oiticica, working at the margins of capitalism, reframed modernist aesthetic issues by translating them directly into life and body. The chapter concludes with an examination of their archives in relation to the reproduction of artworks and to the transition from the archive to the database.[104]

The rapid development of the Internet since 1994, and the increasing number of artists working with digital communications technology has brought new attention to the role of interactivity in electronic media and in emerging digital culture. Interactivity in art, however, is not simply the result of the presence and accessibility of personal computers; rather, it must be regarded as part of contemporary art's natural progression towards immateriality, a phenomenon that is evidenced, for example, in the works of Lygia Clark and Hélio Oiticica.

---

[104]   Lygia Clark's works and archives are housed at the Museum of Modern Art of Rio de Janeiro. Hélio Oiticica's archives are in the Centro Hélio Oiticica, Rio de Janeiro.

Focusing on the circulation of ideas among artists working in vastly different cultures, this chapter explores visual and conceptual parallels between Clark's and Oiticica's sensorial creations from the 1960s and 1970s—masks, goggles, hoods, suits, gloves, capes and immersive environments—and early virtual-reality experiments from the 1960s and 1970s, such as Ivan Sutherland's head-mounted display and the Sayre Glove.[105] Although not technologically based, Clark's and Oiticica's works are also related conceptually to those of artists pushing interactivity in art into new territories. Both in Brazil and elsewhere, their participatory creations continue to yield new meanings.

Although Clark and Oiticica did not focus on technology as a medium for art making, they ventured into it conceptually (Clark's *Four Propositions* of the late 1960s) and experimentally (Oiticica's Cosmococas explorations with drugs and audiovisual media in the mid-1970s). Clark's *Four Propositions*, two involving film and two involving magnets, remained unrealized in her lifetime. I experienced one of those propositions involving magnets in the Museum de Arte Moderna of Rio de Janeiro.[106] Her film proposition "Man at the Center of

---

[105]   Ivan Sutherland's head-mounted display was developed at Harvard University, 1968. His pioneering work with virtual reality, developed around the same time as Clark's masks, was based on the introduction of stereoscopic head-mounted displays. The Sayre Glove was invented by Dan Sandin, Tom DeFanti and Rich Sayre in 1976, and it was used to manipulate three-dimensional forms in real time and virtual space. The glove was developed to provide performance artists with a dynamic, flexible, user-programmable device for creating computer art. The visual and cultural parallels between these and other investigations in art and science are as significant as they are unexplored.

[106]   Lygia Clark, *Lygia Clark* (Rio de Janeiro: Funarte, 1980), 32; and Lygia Clark, "Nostalgia of the Body," *October 69* (Summer 1994), 107-108.

Events" is very similar to Gary Hill's video work *Crux* (1983-1987), in which five cameras were attached to a walking man and the recorded images were shown simultaneously in the shape of a cross. Clark's second film proposition, "Invitation to a Voyage," involved the relation between real and virtual events that take place on the screen and in front of it—an early form of virtual reality. The project is analogous to Jeffrey Shaw's "The Legible City" (1988-1989), in which a stationary bicycle is placed in front of a large screen that projects the roads the cyclist explores. Oiticica's experimentation with Super-8 film and other audiovisual media in the mid-1970s, a period when he lived in New York, mixed art and life in an even more radical way, further enhancing his leisure strategies.[107]

With the exception of a period spanning the 1970s, when Oiticica resided in New York and Clark in Paris, both artists spent their lives in Rio de Janeiro, where they shared a common theoretical ground based in the Brazilian Neoconcrete Art movement.[108] They also shared a fertile artistic dialogue that lasted throughout their careers. Their complementary trajectories were unique and, in both cases, radical. From different perspectives, they contributed to the development of an original

---

[107]   See Ligia Canongia, *Quase Cinema* (Rio de Janeiro: Funarte, 1981), 20-23.

[108]   Concrete Art movements were formed in Rio de Janeiro (*Frente*, formed in 1953) and in São Paulo (*Ruptura*, formed in 1952) as part of the artistic explosion created by rapid industrialization in Brazil during the post-war era. In the visual arts, the theoretical polarization between a "functionalist" tendency in São Paulo and a "vitalist" tendency in Rio de Janeiro resulted in the creation in 1959 of the Neoconcrete Art movement in Rio. Clark and Oiticica were the two most original artists to come out of the Neoconcrete movement. See the "Neoconcrete Manifesto," *October 69* (Summer 1994): 91-95 and also in Dawn Ades, *Art in Latin America* (New Haven, CT: Yale Univ. Press, 1989), 335-337.

vocabulary of interactivity. Clark, merging the body/mind duality, focused primarily on the subjective and psychological dimensions of sensorial experimentation, while Oiticica engaged in sensorial explorations involving social, cultural, architectural and environmental spaces.

Translating Geometric Abstraction into a Language of the Body

Clark and Oiticica questioned representation in art by examining ideas inherited from modern avant-garde movements—Neoplasticism, Constructivism, Suprematism and Concrete Art—that broke with mimesis and assumptions of realism. In the late 1950s, they reframed modernist notions of universal aesthetics by translating them directly into life and body. Weaving a web of relationships around the body's internal and external spaces, they relayed a Modern European geometric abstract tradition to Brazilian vernacular culture. This syncretic process fused two very different traditions—a Western aesthetic canon that privileges vision and metaphysical knowledge, and Afro-Indigenous oral traditions in which knowledge and history are encoded in the body and ritual is profoundly concrete.[109] It must be noted that, in a true syncretic spirit, both traditions have

---

[109]   For a discussion on the concreteness of thought and ritual in oral-based traditions, see Marilyn Houlberg, "Magique Marasa," in Donald Cosentino, ed., *Sacred Arts of Haitian Vodou* (Los Angeles: UCLA Fowler Museum, 1995), 273-274. Holberg's observations about the physicality of ritual in many Afro-American religious ceremonies can illuminate this discussion on the concreteness of Oiticica's and Clark's notion of the body. The artistic traditions of Haitian Vodou have also been recently examined, in the light of a postmodern aesthetic, by M.A. Greenstein, "The Delirium of Faith," *World Art*, No. 3 (1996), 30-35.

always coexisted in Brazilian society at large, but it was not until Oiticica began working that this syncretism was methodically investigated in the visual arts.

In spite of affinities with late 1950s and 1960s counter-cultural movements that also subverted the modernist aesthetic canon, Clark's and Oiticica's works, resisting the labels of Body Art, Conceptual Art, Performance and Happening, stressed the meaning of participation as opposed to its form. Their emphasis on meaning emphasized the experiential aspect of viewer participation. Their resistance to assimilation within mainstream art movements was perhaps less a matter of conceptual incompatibility than a way of emphasizing their original development at the margins of cultural centers, independent of international trends.

In a discussion between Chilean critic Nelly Richard and British critic Guy Brett, Brett illustrated the traditional hierarchical gap between South American and Euro-American artists that Clark and Oiticica struggled to overcome:

> There was an interesting comparison to be made between the exhibition of Hélio Oiticica, a Brazilian artist, which took place in London at the White Chapel Gallery in 1969, and an exhibition of Robert Morris, the American minimalist, which took place at roughly the same time at the Tate gallery. Both exhibitions had a participatory element for the public, and the differences between the two approaches were very fascinating . . . but it was very unlikely at the time that such comparisons would be made because of the immensely greater prestige enjoyed by American artists in London. To have suggested a comparison on equal terms between a famous American and

an unknown Brazilian artist would have been
somehow 'improper,' to borrow Nelly
Richard's use of the notion of propriety. For a
Brazilian writer to have made claims for
Oiticica in direct comparison with Morris
would have seemed the height of naive
nationalism, and even for a non-Brazilian it
would have been difficult. The same naiveté
on the part of the British or North Americans
went, well, unnoticed here.[110]

Clark's and Oiticica's rich and complex legacies were
not only plastic, but also conceptual and existential, expressed in
difficult-to-classify oeuvres that embraced hybrid, contingent
and often, immaterial forms. De-emphasizing visuality, Clark
and Oiticica centered their work on the body, exploring haptic
space through tactile, auditory, olfactory and kinetic
propositions. Their contributions to contemporary art are
relevant not only because of their original development in the
context of Brazilian art, but also because of the unique universal
interactive vocabularies they created and explored with their
manipulable objects, immersive environments and experiential
propositions based on wearable works.

Probing a language of the body and signifying
processes through concrete operations that explored touch,
sound, smell and movement, Clark and Oiticica worked with
life's energy and simple matter, merging perceptual and
conceptual knowledge in ever-changing forms. In his 1968 book

---

[110]   *Witte de With Cahier* No. 2 (June 1994): 90. For further
discussion, see Nelly Richard, "The International Mise-en-scène of
Latin American Art," *Witte de With Cahier*, No. 2 (June 1994): 83;
Nelly Richard, "Postmodern Disalignments and Realignments of the
Center/Periphery," *Art Journal*, No. 51 (Winter 1992); Mari Carmen
Ramírez, "Beyond 'the Fantastic': Framing Identity in U.S. Exhibitions
of Latin American Art," *Art Journal* No. 51 (Winter 1992).

Kinetic Art, London-based critic Guy Brett compared Clark's work with Takis's kinetic sculptures, which introduced the magnet in sculpture as the presence of energy:

> Actual energy is the subject of both their work... Lygia Clark encourages the spectator to use his own energy to become aware of himself. This is something very unusual, and it seems to be a specifically Brazilian contribution to art, a kind of kineticism of the body.[111]

In another article entitled "In Search of the Body," Brett further emphasized Clark's and Oiticica's roots in Brazilian culture, underscoring a special dimension of the body in Brazil:

> Like most such generalizations about national character, perhaps, the 'popular culture of the body' exists both as a stereotype and a truth. It is what makes it possible to read a phrase 'Brazilian elasticity of body and mind' in both a football report and an article on Lygia Clark![112]

This special dimension of sensuality in Brazil poses theoretical challenges both within and without the culture. On one hand, within the Western metaphysical tradition, it reinforces the stereotype that sensuality opposes logos along with other related antinomies such as nature/culture and primitive/civilized. On the other hand, as a source of body

---

[111]   Guy Brett, *Kinetic Art* (London: Studio Vista/Reinhold Art, 1968), 65.

[112]   Guy Brett, "Lygia Clark: In Search of the Body," *Art in America* (July 1994): 61-62.

knowledge inherited from oral traditions, it dissolves the body/mind duality, which was precisely what Clark and Oiticica strove to accomplish.

Clark's and Oiticica's creations, as they changed the traditional role of the viewer and the status of the artistic object, confronting in the process the function of artistic institutions, redefined the identity of the artist and the idea of authorship. Emphasizing viewer participation and material precariousness, their works continue to resist being frozen in museum displays as relics of past actions. Their move from hard to soft and ephemeral materials clearly establishes a historical link to the current immaterial and software-based practices of electronic art. Stressing relational actions, they focused on immaterial exchanges that did not conform to traditional curatorial practices. The challenges still presented by the preservation, re-production, and presentation of their works relates directly to the archive's transformation into a database, accelerated by new media art.

Body-Centered Metaphors of Cannibalism, Carnival, and Hunger

Throughout the twentieth century, avant-garde revolutions often combined a belief in universal aesthetic values with specific national struggles, embracing at the same time aesthetic internationalism and political nationalism.[113] The location of art and archives in particular historical contexts and national histories brings to the forefront political dimensions of art in relation to life, technology and difference, and thus, social

---

[113]   From a European and French perspective, Alain Badiou, *The Century*, (Cambridge, UK: Polity Press, 2007) offers a great exploration of the relations between political and artistic avant-gardes that defined the histories of the twentieth century.

and political struggles involving class, ethnicity, gender, nationality, and colonialism, often at the center of utopian revolutions leading to various authoritarian and democratic regimes. In this struggle, more than a few twentieth-century Brazilian avant-gardes have enlisted popular culture as a rich resource, and employed the body-centered metaphors of cannibalism, carnival, and hunger in order to simultaneously incorporate the foreigner into the familiar and subvert cultural hierarchies that disregarded popular and folk forms of cultural expressions.

"Is an experimental avant-garde possible in an underdeveloped country?" was a provocative question asked by Catherine David, one of the curators of the first large international retrospective of Hélio Oiticica, raising geopolitical questions in art history and criticism.[114] Multiple Brazilian avant-garde artists   subverted "higher" aesthetic values by focusing on folk and popular aesthetics and emphasizing the "lower" senses of touch, taste, and smell suggested by digestive and sexual metaphors.[115]

Some of these subversive tactics are today being employed by new media artists, who in addition to embracing and exploring body-centered metaphors—now in literal ways— are using communication technology to promote new forms of interaction that employ mass communication and mass

---

[114]   Catherine David, "The Great Labyrinth" in *Hélio Oiticica*, Catherine David et all, org. (Minneapolis: The Walker Art Center, 1993): 248.

[115]   Examples include *Anthropophagy* (1928 manifesto), *Neoconcretism* (1959 manifesto), *Cinema Novo* (1962 Aesthetics of Hunger manifesto), and *Tropicalism* (1969 Tropicália album-manifesto). The mixture of elite and vernacular sources in poetry, literature, music, performance, film, visual arts, and architecture often employed carnivalesque and body-centered metaphors of cannibalism and hunger to foster, besides revolutionary artistic practices, notions of identity that were contingent, elastic, and ambiguous.

collaboration on an unprecedented scale. Examples are Wikipedia, Second Life, and Facebook, which facilitate group collaborations to welcome the participation of up to hundreds of thousands.

Gregory Ulmer's *Electracy*—electronic literacy—for instance, argued for, and demonstrated the invention of a new rhetoric and poetic logic for working with a collection of software and web devices, which he has compared to forms of audience participation in oral cultures such as dancing the samba.[116] Ulmer proposed the Brazilian Samba as a model for writing hypertexts. His combination of poststructuralist theory, new technologies, and oral traditions enlisted the Samba dance as a model for creating a new rhetoric: "What is at stake is not the literal dance but the figurative one, changing our cultural style of turning information into knowledge."[117]

Ulmer's reference to the Samba is a welcome reminder that audience participation has a broad history that could include total participation in church liturgies, processions, and especially festivals such as the very pagan yet very sacred four days of *Carnaval* in Brazil. Artists such as Hélio Oiticica have fused these oral traditions—such as the Samba—to misread and reinterpret European Modernism, thus translating geometric abstraction into kinetic body-centered performances. As Ulmer and Oiticica exemplify with generative combinations of very different kinds of knowledge and traditions, one of the

---

[116]   Gregory Ulmer has suggested in his essay "The Object of Post-Criticism," that criticism is now being transformed the same way literature and the arts were transformed by the revolution of the avant-gardes in the first half of the twentieth century. Criticism is belatedly exploring the relationship between critical writing and the subject it 'represents.' Gregory Ulmer, "The Object of Post-Criticism," *The Anti-Aesthetic*, Hal Foster, ed. (Seattle: Bay Press, 1983): 83.

[117]   Gregory Ulmer, "The Miranda Warnings: An Experiment in Hyperrhetoric" in *Hyper/Text/Theory,* George Landow, ed. (Baltimore: Johns Hopkins University Press, 1994): 367.

challenges of media histories is the articulation of art-science-
technology developments in singular and particular examples
but also in the context of a long history of precedents.
Unfortunately some unwritten technologies have disappeared
while others are still downplayed, exoticized, or ignored by
colonialist practices and legacies.[118]

Place: Physical, Conceptual, Cultural, and Technological Dimensions

Whether understood literally or metaphorically, the
concept of place and cultural location in contemporary art is
increasingly complex. In *One Place After Another*, Miwon
Kwon called attention to how site-specific art has changed the
meaning of site: "Site can now be as various as a billboard, an
artistic genre, a disenfranchised community, an institutional
framework, a magazine page, a social cause, or a political
debate. It can be literal, like a street corner, or virtual, like a
theoretical concept."[119] Thus the multiple meanings of site may
include the common understanding of place as topography based
on tangible, measurable descriptions of location, or it may
emphasize topologic and dynamic interactions stressing
immaterial, time-based, and relational art.

Given the complex dimensions of place we wonder: do
place studies work? In relation to nomadic artistic and cultural

---

[118] One important article calling attention to the need for connections
between postcolonial and media theory is Maria Fernandez,
"Postcolonial Media Theory," *Art Journal* 58, no.3 (Fall 1999): 58-73.
See also Diana Taylor, *The Archive and the Repertoire* (Durham: Duke
University Press, 2003), which examines the hegemonic power of text-
based archival sources over performative, oral, and other ephemeral
forms of knowledge.

[119]   Miwon Kwon, *One Place After Another: Site-Specific Art and
Locational Identity* (Cambridge: MIT Press, 2002): 3.

practices, how can one not lose sight of colonial heritages and imperialist economic forces that continue to play a role in how art is made, displayed, received, and historicized? In an interview from 1996, when asked about his nationality Eduardo Kac answered by making it clear how such an apparently simple question was not simple at all: "I don't see myself as an 'American artist' or a 'Brazilian artist,' a 'Holography artist' or a 'Computer artist,' a 'Language artist' or an 'Installation artist.' I prefer not to be bound by any particular nationality or geography. I work with telecommunications trying to break up these boundaries."[120] Like Kac, other artists, curators and theorists who do not work with telecommunication also want to break up these boundaries, as the on-going effort to position works of many Latin American artists within U.S. and European museums and markets can attest.

A recent New York Times article titled "After Frida" examined the role of international curators, collectors, museums, as well as the mass media and the art market in changing the cultural value of many lesser-known Latin American artists.[121] In this effort, the NYT article highlighted the contribution of Marí Carmen Ramiréz, the Latin American curator of the Museum of Fine Arts in Houston. In the article, Robert Storr, the U.S. curator of the 2007 Venice Biennial observed: "This is an interesting situation, where passionate curators, passionate collectors and museums, begin to understand there is a whole rich area that they have overlooked."

Latin American curators, nevertheless, have employed very different concepts and strategies in exposing art from such

[120]   Eduardo Kac quoted by Simone Osthoff "Object Lessons," *Art World*, 1/1996: 18.

[121]   Arthur Lubow, "After Frida," *The New York Times Magazine* (March 23, 2008): 54-61.

a vast and diverse geopolitical area and time period. There has also been a wide range of claims in relation to pioneer accomplishments, and thus various ways of positioning Latin American art in relation to the established canon of Western art. For instance, the exhibition *Global Conceptualism: Points of Origin, 1950s-1980s*, confronted and proposed to reform the Western history of conceptual art, by mounting an exhibition in which the great majority of conceptual artists including pioneers were neither from the U.S. nor from Europe, but from Latin America, Japan and Eastern Europe.

A different strategy was employed by the New York MoMA and by the London Tate Modern. Their displays of Latin American artists, who have been marginal until very recently, tend to promote kinship. Examples are an Hélio Oiticica painted box filled with colorful fabric and dirt next to a stone-and-mirror sculpture by Robert Smithson; a sagging net of woven rice-paper by Mira Schendel next to a rope piece by Eva Hesse; and a Madí Group shaped canvas next to one by Frank Stella.

Regardless of the approach, certain artists, such as the Mexican Frida Kahlo and the Brazilian Hélio Oiticica, have undoubtedly received a lot of attention over the last fifteen years. Oiticica had at least three large retrospectives in the US and Europe, each focusing on a different aspect of his work, and he was included in many other shows.[122] Lygia Clark had one

---

[122]   Solo exhibitions: His first large retrospective was *Hélio Oiticica*, at the Walker Art Center in Minneapolis, MN; it was curated by Katherine David and Luciano Figueiredo among others. It also traveled through three venues in Europe between 1992-1994, Rotterdam: Witte de With Center for Contemporary Art; Paris: Galerie Nationale du Jeu de Paume; Barcelona: Fundación Antoni Tapies; Lisbon: Fundação Calouste Gulbenkian. His second large retrospective of works from the 1970s was *Hélio Oiticica, Quasi-Cinemas*, curated by Carlos Basualdo at the Wexler Art Center and the New Museum of Contemporary Art. It also traveled to Köln, Germany, 2001- 2002. The third comprehensive exhibition was *Hélio Oiticica: The Body of Color* curated by Marí Carmen Ramiréz for the Museum of Fine Arts

large traveling retrospective in Europe and was included in most surveys of contemporary art over the last fifteen years.[123] Edward Sullivan, a scholar of Latin American art at New York University (who was the curator of the large exhibit *Brazil Body and Soul* at the Guggenheim in 2000), commented on the effect these shifts were having on U.S. art history programs:

> Ten years ago students would have gravitated towards art that was figurative, probably Mexican. Now students want to do things that are monochromatic, non-figural, conceptual and geometric or abstract. Oiticica and Clark have replaced Diego and Frida—they are a

---

Houston, Texas and the Tate Modern, London, 2007. Among surveys of Latin American art in which Oiticica was included are the exhibitions: *Latin American Artists of the Twentieth Century*, at the MOMA-NY, 1993; *The Experimental Exercise of Freedom* at the Los Angeles: MOCA, 1999; *Global Conceptualism: Points of Origin, 1950s-1980s* at the Queens Museum of Art in New York, 1999; *Brazil Body and Soul*, Guggenheim Museum, New York, and at the Museo Guggenheim Bilbao, 2001; *Beyond Geometry: Experiments in Form 1940s-70s*, at LACMA, Los Angeles County Museum of Art, 2004; *Inverted Utopias: Avant-Garde Art in Latin America*, at the Museum of Fine Arts Houston, 2004; *Tropicália* at the Museum of Contemporary Art of Chicago, 2005.

[123]   Lygia Clark major retrospective in Europe is titled *Lygia Clark*, curated by Borja-Villel, Manuel J., Nuria Enguita Mayo and Luciano Figueiredo it travelled in 1997-98 between venues in four countries: Société des Expositions du Palais des Beaux-Arts, Brussels; MAC, galleries contemporaines des Musées de Marseille, Marseille; Fundació Antoni Tàpies, Barcelona; and Fundação de Serralves, Oporto. Her work was included in all the group exhibitions listed in footnote 12, besides at least two additional women artist's exhibitions: the *Ultramodern: The Art of Contemporary Brazil*, curated by Aracy Amaral at the National Museum of Women in the Arts, Washington, DC, 1993; and *Inside the Visible: An Eliptical Traverse of 20th Century Art* curated by Katherine Zegher at the MCA in Boston 1997.

power couple in the public imagination the
way Diego and Frida were 10 years ago.[124]

The Oiticica and Clark example is one among many
involving Brazilian, Uruguayan, Argentine, and Venezuelan
artists. Virgilio Garza, The head of Latin American pictures for
Christie's New York observed the Oiticica effect in terms of
dollar figures: "an Oiticica work on paper would go at auction
five years ago for $14,000, and the last time I saw one in a
Brazilian gallery, the asking price was $140,000."[125] That means
a tenfold increase in the last 5 years. In addition, we must not
forget the Latin American artists who achieved international
acclaim "unqualified by nationality," such as Vik Muniz and
Guillermo Kuitca. Of recent interest are also the contemporary
European artists based in Latin America, such as Francis Allÿs
and Melanie Smith in Mexico City, who are bringing new
attention to place and cultural specificity.

---

[124]   Edward Sullivan quoted by Arthur Lubow, "After Frida," *The
New York Times Magazine* (March 23, 2008): 58.

[125]   Virgilio Garza quoted by Arthur Lubow, 61.

Chapter 4.1

Lygia Clark's Trajectory: From Form to Experience

In their development from purely optical-formal concerns to participatory and body-based work, Clark and Oiticica explored the body's multidimensional aspects. Once Clark left one phase of her work, she never returned to it, moving towards ever more immaterial forms. The artistic residue acquired in one phase was always carried into the next, in a process described by Maria Alice Milliet as "traveling with baggage."[126]

In his 1975 book *Art—Action and Participation*, Frank Popper pointed to the new forms of spectator participation as partially responsible for the disappearance of the art object. He named Moholy-Nagy and three others—Israeli artist Yaacov Agam, Roy Ascott and Lygia Clark—as pioneers of the viewer participation movement. Popper described Clark's work as "perhaps the most telling example of the way in which the discipline of optical/plastic research has led to multi-sensorial participation and a type of aesthetic behavior which reconciles the problem of individual and group activity."[127]

Clark's participatory creations spanned nearly 3 decades. The rich interactive vocabulary she developed with objects made from very simple materials began with a series of Neoconcrete geometric sculptures dating from 1960 to 1964.

---

[126]   Maria Alice Milliet, *Lygia Clark: Obra-trajeto* (São Paulo: Edusp, 1992), 179; and also Maria Alice Milliet, "A Obra É O Trajeto," *MAC Revista,* No. 1 (Museu de Arte Contemporânea da Universidade de São Paulo, April 1992): 37.

[127]   Frank Popper, *Art--Action and Participation* (New York: New York Univ. Press, 1975), 13.

These demanded the spectator's manipulation to yield their organic meaning. These sculptures developed into a second series of interactive works centered on the body, roughly divided into two parts: *Nostalgia of the Body* and *Organic or Ephemeral Architectures*. Dating from 1964 to 1968, *Nostalgia of the Body* consists of hoods, goggles, masks, suits, gloves and other objects used by the viewer/participant in individual or two-person sensorial explorations. In these works, viewer participation becomes the focus of attention, while the object remains secondary, existing only in order to promote a sensorial or relational experience. After 1968, these works developed into collective body works Clark titled *Organic* or *Ephemeral Architectures*. In the last phase of her work, lasting from approximately 1979 until her death in 1988, Clark moved even further from traditional definitions of art and artist, employing the whole range of her interactive vocabulary in a form of synesthetic therapy used for emotional healing.

Clark derived the basic defining qualities of her early work from Concrete Art's emphasis on non-representational space and rigorous explorations of line, plane, color and structure. Her reductive black, white and gray paintings from the 1950s explored the complementary aspects of positive and negative space and the boundaries between virtual and literal planes. In the development of her work from painting to interactive sculpture, the issue of edges between painterly illusion and literal space or between the canvas and the frame had a kind of primary importance that was similar to the role that color played for Oiticica. Clark moved into three-dimensional space by way of folding the plane into hinged sculptures that combined geometric shapes and organic movements. This development away from Concrete paintings resulted in a series of Neoconcrete sculptures titled *Bichos* (Animals, or Beasts) from 1959 and 1960.

Clark's geometric *Bichos* needed to be manipulated by the viewer to reveal their organic nature and unfold their multiple configurations. When people asked her how many movements the *Bicho* had, she answered: "I don't know, and you don't know but it knows . . ."[128] Despite their interactive aspect, which also introduced time and movement into the work, the *Bichos* remained formally beautiful objects, and many are displayed today with the attached label "do not touch." Clark, however, emphasizing the importance of the viewer's experience, abandoned the production of art objects altogether to enter a sensorial phase of her work with her *Nostalgia of the Body* series, starting around 1964.

When Clark abandoned the production of the art object, she used the Möbius strip as a metaphor for a new start—a new start that was paradoxically without beginning or end, inside or outside, front or back. Shared by other Concrete artists, her interest in the reversible, continuous, limitless space of the Möbius strip expressed her attraction to non-Euclidian geometry.[129] Clark's new works dissolved the hard edges of the *Bichos* into soft, almost immaterial actions that had no value in themselves, only in relation to the participant were they invested with value. She referred to these action-based works as "propositions." The endless fluid space of the Möbius strip symbolized the path she would pursue for the rest of her career.

Clark's work with the Möbius strip contrasts sharply with Max Bill's sculptures, though they employed the same

----

[128]   Lygia Clark quoted by Lula Vanderlei and Luciano Figueiredo in *Hélio Oiticica and Lygia Clark Salas Especiais, 22 Bienal Internacional de São Paulo* (Rio de Janeiro: Museum of Modern Art of Rio de Janeiro and Museum of Modern Art of Bahia) n.p.

[129]   Max Bill, "The Mathematical Way of Thinking in the Visual Art of Our Time," in Michele Emmer, ed., *The Visual Mind: Art and Mathematics* (Cambridge, MA: MIT Press, 1993), 8. Originally published in *Werk 3* (1949).

form. Bill pursued the visualization of non-Euclidean ideas using traditional techniques as well as permanent materials with noble associations—marble, stone and bronze—in Möbius-strip sculptures to be contemplated by the viewer. Clark, by contrast, defined the concept of endless space as a succession of paradoxical relationships to be directly experienced in the body. Her propositions acknowledged the coexistence of opposites within the same space: internal and external, subjective and objective, metaphorical and literal, male and female. For Clark, the radical new space of the Möbius strip called for new forms of production and communication impossible to explore within traditional artistic categories and practices. For *Caminhando* (Trailings, or Going), from 1964, Clark simply invited the spectator to take a pair of scissors, twist a strip of paper, join it to form a Möbius strip, and cut continuously along the unending plane. *Hand Dialogue*, from 1966, is an elastic band in the form of a Möbius strip that two people use to connect their hands in a tactile dialogue.

Head-Mounted and Sensorial Works: Hoods, Masks, Goggles, Gloves, Body-Suits

The relational aspect of Clark's work in the series *Bichos* became even more apparent in *Nostalgia of the Body*. Brett describes some of Clark's masks from this period:

Clark produced many devices to dissolve the visual sense into an awareness of the body. The *Máscara Sensorial* (Sensorial Hoods), 1967, incorporate eyepieces, ear coverings and a small nose bag, fusing optical, aural and olfactory sensations. A number of helmets hold small movable mirrors in front of the

Ocean Vuong
— the eye is
the loveliest
organism

eyes: one can either look out into the world or back into oneself, or any fractured combination of both. *Máscara-Abismo* (Abyss-Masks), 1967, often blindfolds the eyes. Large air-bags weighted down with stones can be touched, producing the sensation of an imaginary empty space inside the body, and so on.[130]

Clark's hoods, masks, goggles, gloves, suits and other relational objects made of cheap materials provide viewers with experiences that sometimes constrain and sometimes enhance the various senses to activate new connections between them. Clark's gloves, for instance, are made of various materials, sizes and textures. The gloves aim at a rediscovery of touch. Participants use the many combinations of gloves and balls of different sizes, textures and weights, and then hold the balls again with their bare hands.

A similar sensitizing effect resulting from immersion in virtual reality is described by Jaron Lanier:

> There's this wonderful phenomenon where when you're inside a virtual world and if you take off the head-mounted display and look around, the physical world takes on a sort of super-real quality where it seems very textured and beautiful, and you notice a lot of details in it because you've gotten used to a simpler world. So there is actually a sensitivity-enhancing effect.[131]

---

[130]   Guy Brett, "Lygia Clark: In Search of the Body," *Art in America* (July 1994): 61-62.

[131]   Jaron Lanier interviewed by Lynn Hershman Leeson, "Jaron Lanier Interview," in *Clicking In* (Seattle, WA: Bay Press, 1996), 44.

Clark's *Dialogue* goggles from 1968, for instance, restrict the visual field of the two participants to an eye-to-eye exchange, merging interactivity and dialogism, two of the central concerns in Clark's work. Curiously, Ivan Sutherland's pioneering work with virtual reality, developed around the same time, was based on the introduction of the related concept of head-mounted displays. The visual and cultural parallels between these and other investigations in art and science are as significant as they are unexplored. As Myron Krueger has pointed out, "Many aspects of virtual reality including full-body participation, the idea of a shared telecommunication space, multi-sensory feedback, third-person participation, unencumbered approaches, and the data glove, all came from the arts, not from the technical community."[132]

Clark's experiences tend to merge the body's interior and exterior spaces, stressing the direct connection between the body's physical and psychological dimensions. The pure optical emphasis of her geometric abstract paintings from the 1950s are transformed by *Nostalgia of the Body* into sensory explorations of texture, weight, scale, temperature, sound and movement. These sensations are the basis of a non-verbal language employed both in processes of self-discovery and collective explorations among a group of participants. There is a significant conceptual link between these collective explorations and the characteristic of telecommunications art Roy Ascott calls "distributed authorship." Clark's collective creations became her main focus during the period she lived in Paris.

---

[132]   Myron W. Krueger, "The Artistic Origins of Virtual Reality," *SIGGRAPH Visual Proceedings* (New York: ACM, 1993), 148-149.

Collective and Participatory Works

In 1968, as a result of the traumatized public space created in Brazil,[133] Clark moved to Paris. From 1970-1975 she taught at the Sorbonne, returning to Rio in 1977. During this period she developed with her students collective body works that she referred to as *Organic* or *Ephemeral Architecture*. She called these events "rites without myths." She titled one of them *Baba Antropofágica* (translated in English as "Dribble"), meaning literally "Anthropophagic Drool" or "Cannibal Spit."[134]

---

[133]   The year 1968, a historic milestone in many Western countries, marks in Brazil the beginning of an era of state terrorism. The military government in power since 1964 issued the AI-5 (Fifth Institutional Act) signed by military President General Costa e Silva on 13 December 1968. The AI-5 closed Congress and suspended all political and constitutional rights, initiating a period of political oppression and persecution, youth revolt movements and counterculture. The period is the darkest one in the history of the Brazilian military dictatorship. The suspension of human rights opened the way to political persecution, torture and censorship, making it extremely difficult for artists to work. According to Zuenir Ventura, 10 years after the AI-5 was declared, approximately 500 films, 450 plays, 200 books, dozens of radio programs and more than 500 music lyrics, along with a dozen soap opera episodes, had been censored. See Ventura, *1968 O Ano que Não Terminou* (Rio de Janeiro: Nova Fronteira, 1988), 285. The AI-5 was responsible for an artistic and intellectual diaspora (Oiticica and Clark included) and for the fragmentation and isolation of artistic production in Brazil. Cultural production in the 1970s became mostly marginal, isolated from the public and hermetic, communicating only to a small elite. During the 1980s, the country slowly returned to democracy, and little of the irreverent experimentalism of the 1960s survived.

[134]   "Anthropophagia" literally means cannibalism. As employed by the Brazilian avant-garde of the 1920s (the "Anthropophagic Manifesto," by Oswald de Andrade, was published in 1928), anthropophagy called for a cannibalization of European culture in Brazil. It highlighted Afro-Indigenous myths and traditions as superior to the Christian ones, for they were without the double standards of morality and repressed sexuality that artists saw in the patriarchical

For this work, participants placed in their mouths a small spool of colored thread that they unwound directly from their mouths onto another participant who lay stretched out on the ground. The body of the latter was gradually buried under a mottled web of regurgitations. This event was inspired by Clark's dream of an unknown material endlessly flowing from her mouth to create the loss of her own inner substance. The collective vomiting experienced by the group was described by her as the exchange among the participants of psychological content. She also mentioned that this exchange was not pleasurable and that it was about the vomiting of lived experience, which was then swallowed by others.[135]

In the last phase of her work, Clark employed a vocabulary of "relational objects" for the purposes of emotional healing. Objects made of simple materials such as plastic bags, stones, air, shells, water, sand, styrofoam, fabric and nylon stockings acquired meaning only in their relation to the participant. Continuing to approach art experimentally, Clark made no attempt to establish boundaries between therapeutic practice and artistic experience, and was even less concerned with preserving her status as an artist. The physical sensations caused by the relational objects as she used them on the patient's body, communicated primarily through touch, stimulated connections among the senses and awakened the body's memory. Clark's use of relational objects in a therapeutic context aimed at the promotion of emotional balance.

The material simplicity of Clark's propositions confront viewers, however, with very complex issues about art, perception and body/mind relations. Considering participants as

Catholic behavior. The Anthropophagic movement pointed to the "out of placeness" of European ideas in Brazil using inversion, humor and parody as subversive anti-colonialist strategies.

[135]   Lygia Clark quoted by Brett, "In Search of the Body," 62.

Relational aesthetics

subjects-in-process, Clark's work concerns the restructuring of the self through pre-verbal language preceding the enunciation of sentences. Stressing both the present moment and the flux of time, the work is constantly redefined by each participant. Clark's apparently simple creations are, in fact, challenging propositions that ask viewers to infuse the work with their lives and energy. Clark was never concerned with self-expression in art, but instead with the possibility of self-discovery, experimentation, invention and transformation. She began with formalist problems about the exhaustion of representation in painting and ended, three decades later, in a form of synesthetic therapy. In its unique development, Clark's trajectory shows an original inventiveness, a conceptual cohesion and a critical rigor rarely seen in Brazilian art.

Chapter 4.2

Hélio Oiticica: Between Dance and Cinema, Architecture and Music

In the late 1950s, in a process both analogous and complementary to Clark's, Oiticica moved away from optical/pictorial investigations by incorporating time and movement as an active element of his work. His participatory strategies, however, contrast with Clark's in their engagement of the viewer's cultural, social, architectural and environmental space. Color had, in Oiticica's early development, the same importance that edges had for Clark in her transit from pictorial to three-dimensional space. As he explored the relations between color, time, structure and space, Oiticica stated that color frees itself from the rectangle and from representation and "it tends to 'in-corporate' itself; it becomes temporal, creates its own structure, so the work then becomes the 'body of color.'"[136]

Oiticica's creations, like Clark's, became increasingly interactive as he moved from object-based to body-centered works in which viewer participation became the central focus. His Neoconcrete works *Spatial Reliefs* and *Nucleus* (1959-1960)—painted wood constructions suspended away from the wall—expanded ideas inherited from Modernist avant-garde movements, particularly the ideas of Mondrian and Malevitch. These works incorporated color, hue and value in geometrically shaped constructions to be observed from various points as viewers walked around them.

---

[136]   Hélio Oiticica quoted in *Hélio Oiticica*, Guy Brett, Catherine David, Chris Dercon, Luciano Figueiredo and Lygia Pape, eds., (Minneapolis, MN: Walker Art Center and Rotterdam: Witte de With Center for Contemporary Art, 1993), 33.

Continuing to expand color, structure and the act of seeing in space and time, Oiticica surrounded the viewer's body with color in a series of immersive, labyrinth-like painted constructions entitled *Penetráveis* (Penetrables). His series of object-containers, *Bólides* (the Portuguese word for fireball or flaming meteor), are also concerned with the essence of color. The first *Bólides* were glass containers and brightly painted boxes with unexpected openings and drawers filled with pure pigments to be opened by the viewers. The *Bólides* developed from the earliest boxes and glass containers full of pigment, their number expanding throughout the 1960s to reach a total of approximately 50 around 1969. As the *Bólides* evolved, they varied greatly in scale, form, medium and function. They were both constructed and appropriated: some included words or images, some are olfactory, others are homages to people, and some are large structures to be entered and inhabited by the spectator. They all invite perceptual explorations combining, as do many of Oiticica's creations, conceptual sophistication with a raw physicality.

Although *Spatial Reliefs*, *Nucleus*, *Penetráveis* and *Bólides* increasingly invited the active participation of the viewer, it was with his series of wearable creations, titled *Parangolés*, and later on with two installations—*Tropicália* and *Eden*—that Oiticica's work centered itself on the body, promoting through interactivity radically new sensorial experiences. From his colorful painted structures, Oiticica derived his first *Parangolé*, created in 1964. It transformed hard-edged geometric planes into folds of wearable materials made specifically to be danced with. The *Parangolés* were types of capes inspired conceptually by the Mangueira Samba School[137]

---

[137]   *Mangueira* is the name of one of the oldest and most famous favelas (hillside slums) in Rio de Janeiro. The Mangueira Samba school is among the most popular in Rio. See Alma Guillermoprieto, *Samba* (New York: Vintage Departures, 1990). Guillermoprieto lived for 1

to which Oiticica belonged, and they were often made for particular performers. They were, according to Oiticica, "proposals for behavior" and "sensuality tests."

Communicating through experience, the *Parangolés* emphasize the fluidity of life in opposition to any attempt to fix and systematize the world. With this series of uncanny wearable creations made of cheap and ephemeral materials often found on the streets, work and body merge into a hybrid of geometric and organic forms. The participant wearing the *Parangolé* dances with it, exploring kinetically its multiple possibilities.

Expanding the *Parangolés'* architectural origins, Oiticica made two large installations in the late 1960s that he referred to as "experiences." Entitled *Tropicália* and *Eden*, these environments gave a new spatial context to his previous works—*Bólides*, *Penetráveis* and *Parangolés*—by placing them among natural elements such as water, sand, pebbles, straw and plants. Oiticica invited viewers to take off their shoes and inhabit the spaces through leisure activities (such as the simple activity of lying down). The first of these environmental installations, *Tropicália*, was mounted at the Museum of Modern Art in Rio de Janeiro in 1967. *Tropicália* and *Parangolés* are seminal works in the history of Brazilian art.

Addressing the possibility of the creation of a "Brazilian image," *Tropicália* gave name to the emerging Tropicalist movement and opened a cultural discussion that is still far from exhausted.[138] Among the many complex issues

---

year in the favela of Mangueira. In *Samba,* she gives an account of this experience while examining the history and culture of black Brazilians and the social and spiritual energies that inform the rhythms of samba. For a complete history of Rio de Janeiro's samba schools, see Sérgio Cabral, *As Escolas de Samba do Rio de Janeiro* (Rio de Janeiro: Lumiar Editora, 1996).

[138]   Adopting an aesthetic of mixing and contamination, the Tropicalist movement of the late 1960s aggressively combined high and

raised was Oiticica's notion that the myth of "tropicality" is much more than parrots and banana trees: it is the consciousness of not being conditioned by established structures, hence highly revolutionary in its entirety. Any conformity, be it intellectual, social, or existential, is contrary to its principal idea.[139]

Tropicália was the product of an aesthetic of cultural contamination that Oiticica expressed by the writing on one of his Penetráveis: "A Pureza é um Mito" (Purity is a Myth.) In Tropicália, Oiticica made an important reference to the role of the media by placing at the center of his tropical environment a TV set. In 1968, he wrote,

> Entering the main Penetrable, undergoing several tactile-sensorial experiences [...] one arrives at the end of the labyrinth, in the dark, where a TV set is permanently switched on: it is the image which then devours the participants, because it is more active than their sensorial creations.[140]

---

low and industrial and rural cultures, merging political nationalism with aesthetic internationalism and rock and roll with samba. It included all the arts—theater, cinema, poetry, visual arts and popular Brazilian music (especially the works of Caetano Veloso, Gilberto Gil, Gal Costa and Maria Betania). It also inaugurated the "aesthetic of garbage," explored by the second phase of Cinema Novo. It represented a return to cannibalist strategies in the arts, leaving behind the more austere "aesthetic of hunger," with its simplistic Manichean opposition between pure popular nationalism and the alienation of international mass culture. An interesting parallel between Oiticica and the Brazilian filmmaker Glauber Rocha, who became the spokesperson for the New Latin American Cinema, is made by Katherine David in "The Great Labyrinth," in Brett et al., Hélio Oiticica [footnote 1], 248-259.

[139]   Oiticica, "Tropicália" (4 March 1968), in Brett et al., Hélio Oiticica [footnote 1], 126.

[140]   Ibid., 124.

In this text, also titled "Tropicália," and in others, Oiticica called attention to the dangers of a superficial, folkloric consumption of an image of a tropical Brazil, stressing the existential life-experience that escaped this consumption.[141] This concern also informed his second large installation, *Eden*, exhibited at the Whitechapel Gallery in London in 1969 [Fig. 11].

Figure 11. Hélio Oiticica (on the ground) and poet Torquato Neto with the artist's *Parangolés* as part of the Eden experience, Whitechapel Gallery, London, 1969. (Photo courtesy Centro de Arte Hélio Oiticica, Rio de Janeiro). In his immersive environments, which he referred to as "experiences," Oiticica invited participants to take off their shoes and inhabit the space in a leisurely way. Participants explored Eden on their own in an environment made of natural elements, such as sand, straw and water, as well as Parangolés, Bólides, and Penetráveis. The playful aspects of Oiticica's installations emphasize new relations between the

---

[141]   Oiticica's critical views of Brazilian art and culture were condensed in his 1973 article "Brazil Diarrhea," in Brett et al., *Hélio Oiticica* [footnote1], 17-20.

body, space and the leisurely fruition of the work. (Photo John Goldblatt, courtesy of the Projeto Hélio Oiticica, Rio de Janeiro)

Eden, like *Tropicália*, contained different areas that participants could explore in a leisurely way. *Eden* was, however, more abstract in its architectural references than was *Tropicália's* direct allusion to the favela of Mangueira. Avoiding the notion of representation in art, as well as the construction of a tropical image for exportation, the *Eden* experience, similar to the rebirth of the senses enabled by Clark's objects, invited viewers to rediscover pleasurable ways of inhabiting space. Some facets of the *Eden* experience are also present in Roy Ascott's *Aspects of Gaia*, in which viewers placed in horizontal positions within a natural setting playfully explore the conceptual, sensorial and spatial connections of the work.

In 1970, Oiticica received a Guggenheim fellowship and built for the Information show at the Museum of Modern Art (MOMA) in New York 28 *Ninhos* (Nests) that also invited viewer participation in the exploration of space and behavior.

Oiticica's Leisure Strategies: Crelazer and the Supra-Sensorial

Oiticica's contribution to a vocabulary of interactivity expanded Clark's paradoxical explorations of aspects of the body's internal/external space. He created interrelations between the sensual body and the many spatial forms it interacts with. His participatory creations were based on two key concepts that he named "Crelazer" and the "Supra-Sensorial." Crelazer, one of Oiticica's neologisms meaning "to believe in leisure," was for him a condition for the existence of creativity and is based on joy, pleasure and phenomenological knowledge. The second concept, the Supra-Sensorial, promotes the expansion of the individual's normal sensory capacities in order to discover his/her internal creative center. The Supra-Sensorial could be represented by hallucinogenic states (induced with or without the use of drugs), religious trance and other alternate states of consciousness such as the ecstasy and delirium facilitated by the samba dance. For Oiticica, the Supra-Sensorial created a complete de-aesthetization of art underscoring transformative processes. In his words:

> This entire experience into which art flows, the issue of liberty itself, of the expansion of the individual's consciousness, of the return to myth, the rediscovery of rhythm, dance, the body, the senses, which finally are what we have as weapons of direct, perceptual, participatory knowledge [...] is revolutionary in the total sense of behavior.[142]

Oiticica's work fused formal investigation with leisure activities, inviting viewer participation in the creation of "unconditioned behavior."[143] In the cultural context of "the country where all free will seem to be repressed or castrated,"[144] the concepts of Crelazer and the Supra-Sensorial directly defied a pleasure-denying productivist work ethic, subverting it through activities that embraced pleasure, humor, leisure and carnivalesque strategies. Reverie and revolt were never far apart in Oiticica's work, as Brett has pointed out. Leisure for him was first and foremost a revolutionary anti-colonialist strategy.

---

[142]   Oiticica, "Appearance of the Supra-Sensorial" (November/December 1967) in Brett et al., *Hélio Oiticica* [footnote 1], 130.

[143]   Oiticica, untitled text, in Kynaston L. McShine, ed., *Information* (New York: Museum of Modern Art, Summer 1970), 103. See also "Appearance of the Supra-Sensorial" [footnote 1], 127-30.

[144]   Oiticica, untitled text, in McShine, ed., *Information*, 103.

Parangolés: Samba and Interactive Art

Among the many implications emerging from
Oiticica's fusion of geometric abstraction and samba culture is
the return to the mythical, primordial structure of art: a
recreation of the self through an initiatory ritual. Oiticica
described his relation to the popular samba, making reference to
the intense experience provoked by dance:

> The rehearsals themselves are the whole
> activity, and the participation in it is not really
> what Westerners would call participation
> because the people bring inside themselves the
> "samba fever" as I call it, for I became ill of it
> too, impregnated completely, and I am sure that
> from that disease no one recovers, because it is
> the revelation of mythical activity [...] Samba
> sessions all through the night revealed to me
> that myth is indispensable in life, something
> more important than intellectual activity or
> rational thought when these become
> exaggerated and distorted.[145]

For Oiticica, samba was a conduit for the flow of
energy and desire. Samba was a relay, a connector. In an article
from 1965 entitled "Ambiental Art, Post-Modern Art, Hélio
Oiticica," critic Mario Pedrosa traced Oiticica's trajectory from
purely plastic concerns to the existential, the culturally based
and the postmodern. In this process of development from
modern to postmodern art, Pedrosa noticed that Brazilian artists
participated "this time, not as modest followers but in a leading

---

[145]   Oiticica quoted by Brett in "Hélio Oiticica: Reverie and
Revolt" [footnote 1], 120.

role."[146]   According   to   Pedrosa,   Oiticica's   aesthetic
nonconformism   merged   with   his   social/individual
nonconformism due to his Mangueira experience. It was the
artist's initiation into samba that dissolved dualisms and
expanded his work from being object-based to environmentally
based, incorporating in this process the kinetic knowledge of the
body, the structures of popular architecture and the cultural
environment in which they existed. In Pedrosa's words:

> It was during his initiation to samba that the
> artist went from the visual experience in all its
> purity to an experience that was tactile,
> kinetic, based on the sensual fruition of
> materials, where the whole body, which in the
> previous phase was centered on the distant
> aristocracy of the visual, became the total
> source of sensoriality.[147]

Oiticica's premature death at the age of 43 left at loose ends the
many threads he explored, both as an artist and a thinker, in a
meteoric career. His experimental creations assumed a range of
forms that have conceptual rather than formal coherence.
Ranging from paintings to writings, from sculptures and objects
to public actions and events, from constructed immersive
environments to found and appropriated objects and from
wearable works to ambulatory experiences in Rio's bohemian,
marginal and poor neighborhoods, his creations emphasized
sensorial expansion through leisure activities. Oiticica took

---

[146]   Mario Pedrosa, "Ambiental Art, Post-Modern Art, Hélio
Oiticica," introduction to *Hélio Oiticica, Aspiro ao Grande Labirinto*
(Rio de Janeiro: Rocco, 1986), 9-13. Translation mine.

[147]   Ibid., 9.

playfulness seriously, infusing interactivity with what Pedrosa termed "the experimental exercise of liberty."[148]

Tropical Modern: Utopia, Violence, and Political Ambivalence

The relationship between experimental art, utopia, violence and politics at the center of twentieth-century art is the focus of Alain Badiou's *The Century*. Another example from a tropical third-world perspective is Hélio Oiticica's existential and aesthetic references to marginal and outlaw practices. Oiticica revisited the anti-heroic strategies employed by earlier Brazilian avant-gardes, which despite involving a negative aesthetics yielded significant new sensorial explorations and unforeseen spatial possibilities.

Great claims have been made and much faith has been put in art's ability to affect social change, but the defeat of many of Modernity's utopian hopes and dreams—such as the implosion of massive housing projects from the 1960s and 1970s around the world—contributed to undermine its universal assumptions. The concept of utopia, so out of fashion in the postmodern era, despite having inhabited the limbo of the living dead over the past three decades, is perhaps, because of that, a privileged controversial theme in contemporary art. According to David Harvey, author of *Spaces of Hope*, the lack of interest in the utopian tradition in recent times points to the suspicion that there really exists a strict relationship between utopia and

---

[148]   The "experimental exercise of liberty" is a phrase created by Mario Pedrosa and quoted often by Oiticica in his writings. See, for example, Hélio Oiticica, "Experimentar o Experimental," *Arte em Revista* No. 5 (São Paulo: Centro de Estudos de Arte Contemporânea, ed. Kairós, 1981): 50. See also Oiticica, "The Appearance of the Supra-Sensorial" [footnote 1], 127.

totalitarianism.[149] It is not without irony, for instance, that Brasília, built to promote a new democratic society, ended up housing a dictatorship that lasted for a quarter of a century. But it is precisely utopia, understood in a paradoxical way and never fulfilled, that the philosopher Theodor Adorno privileges in art.[150] For him the aesthetic experience is at the center of a critical theory that questions the Enlightenment and the violence of Western rationality; a critical theory that confronts the fascist intolerance towards difference, which led to many twentieth-century political disasters (among them the holocaust).

In Brazil, another example of aesthetics' political ambivalence is *Tropicalismo*; as difficult to define today as it was in 1969, despite the constantly growing international interest in this movement, exemplified by the *Tropicália* exhibit curated by Carlos Basualdo for the Museum of Contemporary Art of Chicago in 2005 and the Bronx Museum of Art in NY, 2006, in addition to the exhibition *Hélio Oiticica: The Body of Color*, at the Museum of Fine Arts, Houston, Texas, between December 2006 and April 2007 and at the Tate Modern, London, in the Summer of 2007.

It is often impossible to separate a negative aesthetics that privileges experimentation, absurd and violent forms from a romantic, idealist, or even functionalist and socially utopian aesthetics. As Oswald de Andrade already observed "at the heart of every utopia there is not only a dream but also a protest." Hélio Oiticica's box-bólide titled *Homage to Cara-de-Cavalo* from 1965, and his flag-poem *Be an Outcast, Be a Hero* from 1967, are both romantic and violent, and have since their creations, raised questions about the relationship between

---

[149]   David Harvey, *Spaces of Hope*, Robert Hullot-Kentor, Trans. (Berkeley: University of California Press, 2000).

[150]   Theodore Adorno, *Aesthetic Theory* (Minneapolis: University of Minnesota Press, 1997).

aesthetics and ethics, and they continue to generate polemics, now with an urgency prompted by gang-related urban violence and the 2006 Presidential elections.

Negative Aesthetics and Anti-Heroes

"We are all in hell. There is no way out, because we don't even know the problem," is the title of the fictional interview with Marcola, the leader of the PCC—Primeiro Comando da Capital [First Commando Group of the Capital]— that the filmmaker and journalist Arnaldo Jabor published in the newspaper *O Globo* on May 23, 2006. In the months that followed, this fake interview circulated in many emails and blogs throughout Brazil, was occassionaly taken to be a real interview with Marcola, and at other times fiction or allegory. What was most impressive about Marcola's words in this conversation with Jabor was the combination of intellectual sophistication with the rationalization for violence. Among literary classics and philosophers supposedly cited by this organized-crime boss, was a reference to Hélio Oiticica's famous quote "Be an outcast, be a hero." In the middle of the interview Marcola states: "Didn't you intellectuals speak of class struggle, of 'be an outcast, be a hero'? Well, here we are! Ha, ha... You never expected these cocaine guerilla fighters, did you?" Jabor's imaginary interview—unfolding in the Nelson Rodrigues's tradition of *A Vida Como Ela É* [life as it is] [151]— continued in this vein for another couple of pages.

----

[151]   Nelson Rodrigues (1912-1980) was born in Recife and lived and worked in Rio de Janeiro. He was a journalist and writer of short stories, novels, and plays, besides being a very controversial author in Brazil. He was loved and hated with the same intensity, labeled both as a genius and a madman, a reactionary and a revolutionary. Rodrigues' writings were reprinted by the Companhia das Letras. For a complete

A second event that year explored the relations between art, media, misery, and violence. On a September morning, the city of Recife awoke covered with posters promoting "Marcola for President and Pedro Correa for Vice President," an urban intervention by artist Krishna Passos that emphasized both political corruption and the politicization of organized crime (documented in the *Folha de Pernambuco* September 20, 2006). The two events—Jabor's fake interview with Marcola, and Passos' Marcola-for-President posters—seemed to ask if there is a direct relationship of cause and effect between art and politics. Can we blame artists like Hélio Oiticica for the increase of violence in Brazilian cities, as does the conservative philosopher Olavo de Carvalho?

In a decade that radically mixed art and life, Oiticica, among others in the 1960s, took the artistic experience beyond the pictorial space and outside the frame and the "neutral" zone of official art institutions. By interpreting Malevich's *White on White* as the limit of painting, the artist translated pictorial questions into life, exploring color and space in time-based performances, which valued the creative potential of samba dance and marginalized urban spaces. Setting color free in space and pursuing a new structure for color, the artist created in 1964, his first *Parangolé*. In the process, Oiticica crossed many aesthetic and spatial boundaries, besides blurring multiple social, racial, and class borders. His redistribution of sensorial experience subverted the Modernist emphasis on the visual sense.

And if Oiticica shortened the distance between the MAM [Museum of Modern Art] and the Mangueira [an important slum in Rio], he rediscovered geometric abstraction in the movement of bodies dancing the samba, while identifying a

biography of Nelson Rodrigues, see Ruy Castro, *O Anjo Pornográfico* (Rio de Janeiro: Companhia das Letras, 1992).

super-sensoriality in states of ecstasy generated by dance rituals, sex, and drugs. Immersed in popular culture he understood marginality and social transgressions to be constitutive parts of an experimental space, that is to say, a radical space in which the rules of behavior are never known beforehand. For Oiticica, this freedom referred not only to aesthetics but ethics as well; as an artist and homosexual, he confronted the morality of a patriarchal Catholic society, as well as the male chauvinism and the racism inherent in Brazilian society. The challenge within the phrase "Be an Outcast, Be a Hero" has its historical and political context in the Military Coup of 1964, and in the subsequent student revolt, where students and non-students fought for freedom of expression and for an alternative, more democratic model of national development. These artistic, social and political ideas were expressed simultaneously and with equal fervor in the plastic arts, cinema, theater, literature, journalism, and popular music.

Oiticica's *Homage to Cara-de-cavalo* [a bandit nicknamed Horse-face] stressed the role of the anti-hero in the modernization of Brazilian culture—from the central character of *Macunaíma*, an important novel from the Anthropophagic movement of the 1920s by Mario de Andrade, to the popular Cordel literature [poetic broadsides] that romanticized Lampião and Corisco [famous outlaws turned popular heroes in the Northeast region of Brazil]. The musical lyrics of Moreira da Silva and Chico Buarque de Holanda also celebrate the anti-hero image of the *Malandro Carioca*, a hustler who used his cunning, charm, and wit to extract creative energy from poverty and oppression, managing to turn around just about any difficult situation. In addition, the bandit-marginal is also at the core of the *Cinema Novo* films such as *Black God, White Devil*, 1964, by Glauber Rocha, as well as the *Boca do Lixo* films such as the *Red Light Bandit*, 1968, by Rogério Sganzerla. The anti-hero is fundamental in the plays and writings of Nelson Rodrigues, and is an integral character in TV soap operas. Thus, the ethical transgressions of the anti-hero are key to multiple avant-garde operations—defacing the ideals of form and beauty—performed throughout the twentieth century by Hélio Oiticica and others. Such ongoing polemics generated by art were recently revisited by the large public outcry after the censoring of the installation *Desenhando Com Terços* [Drawing With Rosary Beads] by Marcia X, in which the late Rio de Janeiro artist placed on the gallery floor multiple rosaries in the form of erect phalluses. This installation was part of the group exhibition *Erótica* at the prestigious CCBB-Rio gallery in April of 2006.

But even when art is openly political, its contribution is first and foremost its ability to maintain in permanent tension the heterogeneity and the difference of all of its constitutive elements–the relations between words, images, and things; as well as the relationship between forms, materials, processes, languages, concepts, senses, and feelings. The connection Oiticica-Marcola questions the artists' ethical and social responsibility, while exposing the raw and cruel lifestyle present in many of Oiticica's works. Viewed in retrospect, Oiticica's celebration of violence seems to romanticize poverty and revolution. Marginality, a liberating project in art of the 1960s, was a result of the search for an experimental space uncompromised by bourgeois values or market interests. This project was derived in part from the "non-object" theory articulated by the critic Ferreira Gullar in 1960, in continuity with the Neoconcrete ideas that conceived art beyond notions of representation. In other cultural contexts, the combination of art and politics also led to the same anti-representational impulse. An example is the media intervention by the *Tucumán Arde* group within the labor movement in Rosário, Argentina, in 1968. A further example against mimesis can be found in the Minimalist movement, also known as ABC, or literalist art, theorized by artists such as Donald Judd and Robert Morris in New York, in 1966.

The experience of ecstasy and violence present in some of Oiticica's works might be closer to the experience of the sublime, which includes the non-rational and the irrational, intrinsic parts of the experience of beauty initially conceptualized by Edmund Burke in the eighteenth century. In the lyrical and ecstatic dimension of Oiticica's works there is the desire to dissolve the separation between subject and object through joyous liberation and the "experimental exercise of freedom."

But contrary to Adorno's horror of the cultural industry, we today believe that contemporary art must indeed explore all cultural forms, including those taken from, and existing within the mass media. Context is content, and the blurry lines between representation and simulation inevitably reject the Modernist universal claim to aesthetic purity and autonomy. An example of this Modernist bias is the notion that Cubism was responsible for the radical invention of collage, propagated as an autonomous artistic development, rather than a pictorial appropriation of methods already employed in the advertising industry since the second half of the nineteen century. In Brazil, the subversive body-centered metaphors of cannibalism, carnival, and hunger, which have been at the core of many twentieth-century revolutionary aesthetics, can further dislocate high and low sensibilities by subverting the optical and aural senses with digestive and sexual metaphors, thus promoting a cannibalization and a carnivalization not far from the aesthetics of cultural remix.

Sampling and remix, born from collage, film montage, jazz and hip hop—radicalized and facilitated by the widespread access to digital technologies—continues to build upon the political ambivalence of many twentieth-century avant-garde practices. With dizzying speed—from Oswald's emphasis upon the "contribuição milionária de todos os erros" [the rich contribution of all mistakes] to Fernando and Humberto Campana's street based furniture designs, such as their *Favela Chair*—the logic of cultural remix tends to leave the material, metaphorical, and political fault-lines of collage and sampling exposed.

Among the failures of the utopian and revolutionary Modernist ideals were the many attempts to deny the notion of art as commodity by the 1960s neo-avant-gardes. Even though documents of performances and other immaterial experiences were in the end reintegrated into the art market, the broadening of the artistic experience into multifaceted relationships between art, commerce, and the media, is today producing more complex and less innocent works. Art and the artist are not above the good and the bad in a self-referential world, but art's own logic and ethics promotes a critical renovation of culture, including the questioning of the nature and the function of art itself, as well as the limits of institutions and other artistic and media venues.

Contrasting with Modernity's utopias, and yet building upon some of their political ambivalence, contemporary artists today are both critical of the values of global corporate capitalism, and yet they thrive within the international media celebrity system. Such is the case of sound artist Paul Miller, a.k.a. DJ Spooky, an important innovator and theorist of the remix.[152] Spooky's form of resistance, which openly embraces new technologies to challenge racism and collapse disciplinary and social hierarchies, is aware of technology's military and corporate implications, while seeking to further the blurring of

---

[152] Paul Miller, *Rhythm Science* (Cambridge, MA: MIT Press, 2004), and also edited by the same author, *Sound Unbound*, (Cambridge, MA: MIT Press, 2008).

the lines between representation and simulation. The new meanings produced by his performances merge experimental and functional art, avant-garde and kitsch spectacle, sampling and copyright, open source and capitalist-for-profit. Whether practiced by twentieth or twenty-first century artists, in the tropics or elsewhere, the political ambivalence inherent in the aesthetics of cultural remix does not necessarily lead to utopian or dystopian experiences, but often to a critical and "experimental exercise of freedom."

Chapter 4.3

From Body Art to Database Art

Figure 12. Nildo da Mangueira with *Parangolé 4 Capa 1* (1964).
Exhibition *Hélio Mangueira Oiticica*, UERJ, 1990. Photo: Andreas
Valentim courtesy of the Projeto Hélio Oiticica, Rio de Janeiro)

From the visual exploration of pictures to sensual and
experiential artworks involving touch, smell, taste, hearing and
movement, the participatory legacies of Lygia Clark and Hélio
Oiticica changed how the archive stores, reproduces and enacts
ephemeral art experiences. In part, their short-lived artworks
were created to resist the notion of art as commodity. But as

Miwon Kwon observed, they ended up entering the art market anyway, if a bit later, and even in some cases with the help of the artists themselves. Kwon argued that in many 1960s performances, the art object might have been gone, but the structure of exchange between artists and audiences was not essentially altered, despite audience participation. She pointed out that dematerialization of art was not the same thing as anti-commodification, given that the art experience and its instructions, scores, and relics often became the new artistic commodity. And in many cases, the dematerialization of art paradoxically produced the commodification of the artist him/herself. [153] Therefore, what counts as artistic labor has been radically redefined by the 1960s avant-gardes, while their emphasis on experience in art changed the functions of the archive to include the re-production of artworks.

The fleeting nature of many of Clark's and Oiticica's works requires their reproduction for different exhibitions, creating multiple "originals" while also opening the archive to the possibility of recombination [*Fig. 12*]. Thus changing the archive's former reliance on a collection of original artworks and transforming the archive into a database. This transformation from an archive of original artworks, such as Picasso's paintings, for instance, to the archive as a repository of concepts to be produced and reproduced at a later date, either by the artist or the curator, suggests a new status and function for the archive, one that positions it as a database. But today, even without an emphasis upon participatory art, the changes involving the archive increasingly relate to art exhibitions, as contemporary artists approach exhibitions, no longer as the display of finished works but as a time-based medium, or the staging of a living artwork, in sum, as part of a larger process or as a starting point to go somewhere else. Thus, exhibitions are

---

[153]   Based on my notes from Miwon Kwon's lecture at the Palmer Museum of Art, Penn State University on March 23, 2005.

frequently on-going and without an end in sight. Examples are the exhibition *History Will Repeat Itself*, and Eduardo Kac's *Rabbit Remix*.

The development of the archive of ephemeral artworks into a database—such as Lygia Clark's masks and props for sensorial experiences, or Oiticica's blueprint instructions for his *Cosmococa* installations, which were never realized in his lifetime[154]—suggests a comparison with another important transformation of the archive based upon a scientific and statistical approach to information that allows for permutation. The scientific organization of archives into databanks was part of the continuous development of the instrumentalization of reason in Western thought, which produced both science and modern technologies and, as Heidegger pointed out in the "Question Concerning Technology," rather than anything mechanical, is ultimately the actual essence of technology which Heidegger termed *Gestell*, enframing—"an utter availability and sheer manipulability of nature's resources that ultimately includes men themselves."[155]

The generative and recombinant nature of databanks allowing for multiple uses in media arts and opens further inquiry into the archive's changed ontology, as Wendy Chung

---

[154]   The first five *Cosmococas* multimedia installations conceived and envisioned by Hélio Oiticica and Neville D'Almeida in New York in 1973, were created for two exhibitions: *Hélio Oiticica, Quasi-Cinemas,* curated by Carlos Basualdo at the Wexler Art Center and the New Museum of Contemporary Art, also traveled to Köln, Germany, 2001- 2002; and the exhibition *Cosmococa: Programa in Progress: Hélio Oiticica and Neville D'Almeida*, curated by César Oiticica Filho, Paulo Herkenhoff and Kátia Maciel. Rio de Janeiro: Projeto Hélio Oiticica, and Buenos Aires: Centro de Arte Contemporânea Inhotim and Museo de Arte Latinamericano de Buenos Aires, 2005.

[155]   Martin Heidegger, "Question Concerning Technology," in *Basic Writings*, David Farrell Krell, Trans. (New York: HarperCollins, 1993), 311-341.

observed in relation to the generative "ghostly" nature of digital archives (if not literally alive, then at least no longer dead); and as Eduardo Kac's performances of the archive suggest, by opening up further ground for inquiry and research.

Chapter 5

Paulo Bruscky: From Mail Art to the Archive as Installation Art

REALLY?

Networks have no centers, only nodes. Much of the experimental art of the 1970s and 1980s were developed in points of intersection, cultural hubs, distributed around the world. This chapter examines one of those hubs, located in Recife, Brazil, through the early works of Paulo Bruscky. Performing outside traditional art institutions and practices, Bruscky used the mail system to forge complex relations between place and space while transforming art and life through cultural activism. During this period, he approached art without regard for national borders or the categorical boundaries of traditional media. With a consciousness of art as an ideological system constituted and validated in large part by official institutions—the studio, art market, museum, gallery, art criticism, art history—Bruscky eschewed traditional venues and objects, opting instead, from the beginning of his career, to invent new ones.

DIY FOREVER

This chapter discusses his early works in relation to the political climate in which they operated. Born in 1949, Bruscky's works from the 1970s contributed not only to the aesthetics of remote action and interaction, but confronted the political repression of the era. From 1968 to the late 1980s, Brazil was marked by a deprivation of public freedoms imposed by the military dictatorship, first installed with a coup in 1964. Bruscky engaged with art at a significant turning point in the Brazilian political-cultural context responding to the political repression of the early 1970s. For almost a decade his work has undergone its first wave of national recognition.[156] Only in the recent increasingly pluralistic art scene have his accomplishments begun to receive deserved recognition.

Bruscky shares with other Brazilian artists such as Eduardo Kac a sense of responsibility in his engagement with art, which he has advanced primarily not as the production of physical objects, but rather as the examination of ideas, relationships, contexts, and consciousness. The live interventions he created in the 1970s were an integral part of the social, cultural, and political networks that give art meaning. During this period Bruscky sharpened the edge of artistic discourse by creating critical, humored, and performative cultural interventions—the very practice of freedom. This chapter examines his works prior to and in relation to the exhibition of his archive as an installation at the São Paulo Bienal in 2004, which was the focus of chapter one.

---

[156]   Paulo Bruscky's work has recently been showcased in various Brazilian exhibitions, roundtable discussions, and important articles such as Ricardo Basbaum's "O Artista Como Curador," in *Panaroma da Arte Brasileira 2001* (São Paulo: Museu de Arte Moderna de São Paulo, 2001); and Cristina Freire, *Paulo Bruscky: Arte, Arquivo e Utopia* (São Paulo: Companhia Editora de Pernambuco, 2006), and the same author's *Poéticas de Processo* (São Paulo: Iluminuras, 1999). A large retrospective exhibit of his work was held at the Observatório Cultural Malakoff in Recife in 2001. Bruscky's videos were screened in 2002 in Recife (Fundação Joaquim Nabuco), Curitiba (Cinemateca de Curitiba), and Rio de Janeiro (Agora). The information about Bruscky's work included in this chapter is based on an interview with the author on May 27, 2002, at Bruscky's Torreão studio in Recife, Brazil.

Aesthetics of Circulation and Reproduction

One of Brazil's darkest periods of state political oppression began in 1968 and extended through the 1970s. During those years, making art, and especially experimental art, was a difficult and dangerous proposition.[157] Nevertheless, artists continued to resist authoritarian structures by pushing the boundaries of experimentation and the limits of public freedom. They often chose to circulate their works outside official artistic institutions, perceived by many as being in agreement with the oppressive governmental regime. Many artists, such as Hélio Oiticica and Lygia Clark, chose to spend most of the seventies in exile, continuing to emphasize the participatory, sensorial explorations they had embraced in the 1960s.[158] In 1970 in Rio de Janeiro, Cildo Meireles printed the message *Yankees Go Home* on Coca-Cola bottles—a symbol of American imperialism—and stamped the question *Quem Matou Herzog?* (Who Killed Herzog?)[159] on Cruzeiro notes, returning both

---

[157]   The year 1968 marks the beginning of an era of state terrorism in Brazil. On December 13 of that year, the military government issued the AI-5 (Fifth Institutional Act), signed by military President General Costa e Silva. The AI-5 closed Congress and suspended all political and constitutional rights, opening the way to political persecution, torture, and censorship. Following their interruption by a military coup in 1964, presidential elections were not held again until 1989.

[158]   For Hélio Oiticica's 1970s production, see Carlos Basualdo, ed., *Quasi-Cinemas* (Columbus, Ohio: Wexner Center for the Arts, 2001). For Lygia Clark's work and writings, see Manuel J. Borja-Villel, Nuria Enguita Mayo, and Luciano Figueiredo, eds., *Lygia Clark* (Barcelona: Fundació Antoni Tàpies, 1998).

[159]   Vladimir Herzog was a São Paulo investigative journalist who was arrested by the security forces and later found hanging in his cell. The government stated that his death was "a suicide," a claim few, if anyone, accepted. Most people believed he was tortured to death by the Brazilian police and government.

bottles and currency to circulation. These works were part of Meireles's series *Insertion into Ideological Circuits,* which employed systems of currency and commodity circulation and distribution to carry subversive political messages. In these works, the scale of the intervention was not the point (the message on a Coke bottle can be seen as a message in a bottle thrown into the sea), but the performance of an act designed to "give voice to the void," as art critic Paulo Herkenfoff has pointed out.[160]

In Recife, on Brazil's northeast coast, Bruscky found in the Mail Art movement an alternative venue for art making, participating in shared networks of ideas and gestures of resistance that linked national and international artists. The Mail Art movement bypassed the market of artistic commodities, as well as the salons and biennials that treated art exhibitions like beauty pageants. Bruscky's work engaged with Fluxus's concepts of fusion of art and life. His interest in processes of circulation, reproduction, and distribution yielded performances and interventions that may not always have looked like "art," or even been counted as "art," but that without doubt generated a new thinking that traditional art practices could not articulate.

Mail Art: To and from Recife

Over the last three decades, Bruscky's work has taken many forms and employed various materials, sites, and aesthetic strategies. For him, the great network started with Mail Art in the 1960s. Despite the earlier pioneer examples—from Stephane Mallarmé's poem-addresses on envelopes to Marcel Duchamp's postcards—only in 1960, with Fluxus artists, and in 1962 with

---

[160]   Paulo Herkenhoff, "The Void and the Dialogue in the Western Hemisphere," in *Beyond the Fantastic,* ed. Gerardo Mosquera (London: inIVA, 1995), 69–73.

Ray Johnson, according to Bruscky, did the international Mail Art movement begin to fully employ the mail system as medium. Mail Art continued to develop throughout the 1970s, connecting Latin American artists not only with one another, but with artists from the Gutai group in Japan and Fluxus artists in the United States and Europe. Bruscky corresponded with Johnson, Ken Friedman (with whom he performed in New York), and Dick Higgins, among others.

Bruscky initially became involved with the Mail Art movement in 1973, not only as a participant, but also as a promoter, organizing international Mail Art exhibits in Recife in 1975 and 1976. Bruscky's archives contain fifteen thousand mail art works and are today an important source of documentation of the movement. The First International Mail Art Exhibit in Brazil, organized by Bruscky and Ypiranga Filho in 1975 in Recife's central post office, was closed by censors minutes after its opening (many Latin American participants included messages denouncing state violence and censorship). Brazil's Second International Mail Art Exhibit in 1976, organized by Bruscky and Daniel Santiago, and again sponsored by the central post office, showcased three thousand works from twenty-one countries. This exhibition was also closed by the police immediately after opening. It was seen only by a few dozen people. Bruscky and Santiago were dragged off to prison by the federal police and detained incommunicado for ten days. The majority of the works in the show were returned to the artists by the police after thirty days; many were damaged, and others were confiscated indefinitely as evidence.

Bruscky was jailed three times, in 1968, 1973, and 1976. After 1976 he received death threats over a period of six months and was constantly followed by the police until he denounced this situation as the theme of a solo show in a Recife art gallery, making public a threat he had been, up to that point, undergoing privately. He was never associated with a political party, and his militancy was first and foremost cultural and artistic, embracing art as "the experimental exercise of freedom."[161]

Communication at a distance, public participation and circulation—concepts central to the Mail Art movement—playfully deployed the rules and regulations of the international mail system, as in Bruscky's series *Sem Destino* (Without Destination and/or Destiny), 1975–1982. Bruscky created artist stamps and messages on envelopes, such as *Hoje a Arte é esse Comunicado* (Today Art Is This Message), a sentence he often stamped on works; used postcards, telegrams, telex; and devised chain letters that produced multiple editions and often boomeranged back to the sender. Though supported by a few art institutions, Mail Art was resisted by others who in the early 1970s displayed no interest in conceptual experimentation. An example of the latter was the rejection by the jury of Bruscky's 1973 installation proposal, which he sent in the form of a telex to the 30th Salão Paranaense (a show in the south of Brazil). The missive proposed the following three installations as his entry: the first, a formless pile of all the packing materials from the other artworks arranged in a corner of the exhibition space; the second, all the materials used by the museum cleaning staff (brooms, buckets, water, rags) hanging one meter above the floor; the third, a display over a chair of all the materials used in the installation of artworks (screws, nails, hammers, etc.), along with the title *Don't Touch! These Objects Are Being Exhibited.*

Through Mail Art, Bruscky promoted public happenings, along with encounters

---

[161]   The forward-looking Brazilian art critic Mario Pedrosa used this expression in the 1960s to describe the experimental works of Oiticica, Clark, Lygia Pape, Antonio Manuel, and others. Rina Carvajal and Alma Ruiz, eds., *The Experimental Exercise of Freedom* (Los Angeles: MOCA, 1999).

among strangers brought about by the correspondence network. An example was the happening Bruscky created in 1977 for the Ricerche Inter/Media Centro Autogestito di Attivita Espressive in Ferrara, Italy. Titled *Re-Composição Postal* (Postal Recomposition), it promoted an encounter among twenty-seven of Ferrara's citizens, who received by mail a section of a work divided by Bruscky into twenty-seven parts to be reassembled by the recipients.

Mental Space, Aural Space, Aero Space: The Sky Is the Limit

While involved with Mail Art, Bruscky simultaneously explored various performance, cinematic, aural, and electronic aesthetics. The multimedia he examined in the 1970s included reproductive technologies (electrography, blueprinting, and fax), along with experimental film and video. In 1970, while working as a hospital administrator, Bruscky developed sound poems based on patients' utterances, moans, and screams and created a series of "drawings" using electrocardiogram, electroencephalogram, and X-ray machines. These graphic images were later incorporated in Mail Art envelopes and in various performances, including those with fax machines. Bruscky also created sound poems and compiled sound works by other artists, including John Cage, broadcasting them on a mainstream Recife radio station during the winter art festivals of 1978 and 1979.

Emphasizing connections among art, science, and technology, the artist quotes Santos Dumont, the Brazilian inventor and father of aviation, observing that "whatever one man imagines, others can achieve." For Bruscky, it is important to place art in the realm of visionary scientific and technological inventions. This wider cultural horizon for artistic creation allowed him the freedom to pursue large-scale, open-ended projects, such as his 1974 proposition for the creation of artificial aurora borealis (to be produced by airplanes coloring cloud formations). Bruscky placed ads in newspapers to both document and circulate the project while looking for sponsors. These appeared in the *Diário de Pernambuco* (Recife), September 22, 1974; in the *Jornal do Brasil* (Rio de Janeiro) December 29, 1976; and in the *Village Voice,* May 25, 1982. The creation of artificial auroras was finally realized in 1992, not by Bruscky, but by the U.S. National Aeronautics and Space Administration (NASA) as part of environmental research. Approximately sixty artificial mini-auroras were created by employing electron guns to fire rays at the atmosphere from the space shuttle *Atlantis.* [162]

From Copy Art to Teleart: Duplication and Transmission, "Today Art Is This Message"

Bruscky's exploration of reproductive technologies in the 1970s and early 1980s, from the use of stamps in Mail Art to photocopiers and fax machines, was rooted in his training as a photographer and his engagement with visual poetry. His performances with photocopiers shared with artists of the 1960s and 1970s an antirepresentational attitude toward art making, a desire to short-circuit the relations between original and copy, as well as the work's inside/outside boundaries. In this process of unhinging modes of production, representation, and circulation, he underscored how the context in which art operates frames and produces meaning. His criticism of originality in Xerox Art (the name photocopy art received in Brazil) also explored ironically the specificity of the medium, as Bruscky employed reductive and additive processes with a playful and poetic sensibility that

---

[162]   William Harwood, "Um vôo em que tudo deu certo," *Jornal do Commercio* (Ciência/Meio Ambiente, Recife), April 3, 1992.

expanded the limits and functions of the photocopier. He adjusted and altered the various parts of the machine to orchestrate series of images produced with cinematic sensibility. He expanded the machine's narrow depth of field by using mirrors and slide projections below and above the photocopier's flat bed. From his prolific cycle of photocopy art, Bruscky made three Xerofilms, eventually part of his total experimental production of about thirty short films and videos. His Xerofilms were made with stop motion from thousands of Xerox copies produced in performances [*Fig. 13*].

Figure 13. Paulo Bruscky in the act of his "Xeroxperformance" at the Universidade Católica de Pernambuco-Recife, 1980. This performance generated 1,350 photocopies that were filmed in stop motion, creating an experimental film animation under the same title. (Photo provided by the artist)

For his second Xerofilm, for instance, Bruscky set fire to a photocopier, which documented its own destruction in 25 seconds. For this body of work with photocopiers Bruscky, received a Guggenheim Fellowship in 1980 and spent the ensuing year working in New York and various cities in Europe.

Fax Art was another means of mediating distances, conflating the experience of Mail Art with that of Xerox Art while enabling new performances from afar. The first artistic fax transmission in Brazil was executed between Bruscky in Recife and Roberto Sandoval in São Paulo on October 31, 1980. The documentation of this first transmission was exhibited in Arte Novos Meios/Multimeios (New Media/Multimedia Art) at the Fundaccio Armando Alvares Penteado (FAAP) in São Paulo in 1985.[163] In other fax performances Bruscky incorporated the 1970 electrocardiogram "drawings" of his brain waves and the graphic recorded heartbeats of his electrocardiograms in "direct transmissions of thought" he referred to as *Cons-ciência da Arte* (a title that doesn't translate readily into English but refers to both art's consciousness and science). For Bruscky, the machines registered his "direct drawing process" documenting in graphic form, his thoughts and feelings, brain and heart activity.

Bruscky has maintained an active presence in Recife's cultural scene for more than three decades and continues to work as an artist, curator, and archivist. In works from the 1970s, he approached art with a new agency that is becoming increasingly important to a younger generation of artists. Whether working with the mail system or planning sky art interventions in which

---

[163]   Curated by Daisy Pecinini, this exhibit was one of the few that in the 1980s focused on emergent art engaged with technology. Among other artists, Bruscky participated with his three Xerofilms, in addition to his fax art documentation from the 1980s and a new fax transmission for the show. Kac exhibited three of his holopoems, "Holo/Olho," from 1983, and "OCO" and "Zyx," from 1985.

airplanes paint the clouds, his performances erupted into public spaces without the sanction of traditional institutions or curatorial authorities, continuously expanding the boundaries of art beyond its traditional frame and producing alternative sites for artistic creation and circulation. Bruscky worked both within and without art institutions, acting directly on the urban environment and often employing the media—such as newspapers, billboards, and radio stations—as venues, artistic media, and forms of documentation. His experimental practices reaffirm art's critical and activist edge while becoming a lesson for critical theorists and independent curators in their rethinking of the boundaries between art making, critical writing, and curatorial practices. In his engagement from Mail Art to Fax Art, Bruscky's work ignored physical distances, performing experimental actions that continuously locate art in the utopian space beyond the medium and beyond national and geographical boundaries.

What Kind of Documental Collection is Formed When the Artist is the Archivist?

Bruscky's archive in Recife has been a depository of among other things many documents of the mail art movement. The archive contains many books, Bruscky's collection of about fifteen thousand works of mail art, newspapers, artists' books, films and videos, sound poems, the artist's own works, photographs, and research. For a couple of decades this content was informally made available to other artists and researchers. The decision to display his archive as it exists in a two-bedroom apartment, emphasized its form and the architecture of the space that houses it. In addition it highlights the artist as researcher, as a cultural activist who was also responsible for preserving the memory of a movement that was never absorbed by the market and in large part was ignored by official institutions. In the end, the exhibition of Bruscky's archive as an art installation suggests that a documental collection of the Mail Art movement is indistinguishable from Bruscky's conceptual ouevre. Therefore, at least on occasion, the archive and history are inside the realm of art and we cannot separate between fiction and non-fiction.

Chapter 6

Eduardo Kac: Networking, Implanting, and Remixing the Archive

Over the course of two decades Eduardo Kac's hybrid networks connected, in real time, disparate and distant elements. They have also offered new insights into art while leading the artist in 1999, to the literal creation of new hybrid life forms. By changing habitual ways of seeing and communicating, Kac's networks and transgenic creations continuously challenge our understanding of the "natural" environment as well as of the environment of art. They explore what the French philosopher Jacques Rancière termed the "distribution of the visible, the sayable, and the possible."[164] This chapter offers a brief overview of Kac's development from the early 1980s.

By converging art, science and technology, with communication theory, philosophy and poetry, the artist produces unusual connections such as those between language, light and life. Insightful and experimental, Kac's work suggests alternative ecologies neither by denouncing climate change and environmental disasters nor by calling attention to monstrous threats produced by manipulation of DNA information. The dimensionalities and temporalities explored by his networks— both human and non-human—examine the wider ecological questions posed by Félix Guattari's *The Three Ecologies*, a manifesto that called upon activists "to target the modes of

---

[164]   "Art of the Possible" Fulvia Carnevale and John Kelsey in conversation with Jacques Rancière, *Art Forum* (March 2007): 256-259.

production of subjectivity, that is, of knowledge, culture, sensibility, and sociability."[165]

Prompting a continuum between nature and culture, between species, and among the senses, Kac's work questions the structures, mediations, and ultimately the supremacy of vision in art, while promoting synesthetic experiences that rearticulate individual consciousness within social, cultural, and finally environmental realms. In addition, his work addresses issues of spectatorship by emphasizing participatory action and two-way communication. His hybrid networks of physical and virtual spaces dislocate audiences by immersing them in environments that examine how vision, touch, hearing and voice are facilitated and constrained by the structures and mediation of new technologies. In his networked environments dialogical communication among humans, animals, plants, microorganisms and machines is never given, but instead must be construed by participants word-by-word, frame-by-frame.

Never purely visual, always impurely polysemic, and disregarding traditional disciplinary boundaries, the artist's works are neither easy to classify nor to locate. When I first interviewed Kac more than a decade ago; curious about his fluency in at least four languages (English, Portuguese, Spanish and French), I began by asking him about his nationality. He answered that his work was not about location but connectivity: "I prefer not to be bound by any particular nationality or geography. I work with telecommunications, trying to break up these boundaries."[166] For him, identity and location are never fixed, but vectors in the production of subjectivity that his work explores.

---

[165]   Félix Guattari, *The Three Ecologies*, (London: Athlone Press, 2000), 49.

[166]   Kac quoted in Simone Osthoff, "Object Lessons," *World Art,* no. 1 (1996): 18.

Kac began his career in Rio de Janeiro with wildly transgressive poetry performances on Ipanema beach (1980-82). In 1983, seeking to create a new language for poetry out of the fluidity of light, the artist found in holography a new medium for art making. His holopoems (1983-1993), which use light as an immaterial writing environment, depend on the location of the body of the viewer in space for the construction of their syntax and semantic meanings. Kac approached holography as a time-based medium, where not only the eyes, but the whole body of the viewer is activated.

Parallel to his holopoems, since 1985, Kac has been exploring communication at a distance in complex interactive works connected via telecommunication systems—at first videotexts, videophones, and telerobotics—then through more complex networked events taking place on the Internet. In these telepresence works communication was not only mediated by hardware and software but was negotiated among multiple participants, at times animals of different species, such as in his 1994 *Essay Concerning Human Understanding*, in which a dialogue took place through the network between a plant in New York and a bird in a gallery in Lexington, Kentucky. Many viewers were skeptical. Was the work a practical joke? Could a real phone dialogue take place between a plant and a bird? Was this a poetic metaphor or a real and literal conversation?

Actual communication involving not only different species, but also multiple institutional nodes both private and public is central to the artist's aesthetics. Kac's telepresence events emphasize real time over real space, linking humans, animals, plants and machines in several nodes of observation and participation worldwide. Furthermore, his telepresence events underline the spatial dislocation of vision into multiple points of view. Between Kac's telepresence events with the *Ornitorrinco* telerobot (1989-1996) and the transgenic creations he started in 1999, are a number of complex telepresence installations and performances that expanded the artist's examination of interspecies and remote communication, including human-machine exchanges: *Teleporting An Unknown State* (1994-96); *The Telepresence Garment* (1995-96); *Rara Avis* (1996); *A-Positive* (1997); *Time Capsule* (1997); *Uirapuru* (1996-99); and *Darker Than Night* (1999).

Commenting on a series of telepresence works created with his telerobot *Ornitorrinco* (1989-1996), Kac stated: "What the telepresence installation with the Ornitorrinco telerobot is all about is to metaphorically ask the viewer to look at the world from someone else's point of view. It's a non-metaphysical out-of-body experience, if you will."[167] This positional exchange between viewers and the point of view of the telerobot is further expanded in *Rara Avis*, 1996, where the artist employed VR technology and multiple Internet protocols to displace the viewer's gaze into the body of a robotic macaw while turning that gaze upon viewers themselves.

A transitional work between Kac's telepresence events and his bio art is *Time Capsule* from 1997, in which the artist examined issues of memory and digital archives, which literally entered the artists' body through the implantation of a microchip in the artist's ankle. The chip information was then interactively stored in a data bank in the U.S. while being simultaneously broadcast on television and on the Web. Like his early performances on Ipanema beach, holopoems and telepresence events, Kac's bio artworks continue to explore communication processes, as well as new ways of seeing, writing, reading, and speaking. Translation and inscription are especially prominent in his transgenic Creation Trilogy—*Genesis* (1999), *GFP Bunny* (2000), and *The Eighth Day* (2001)—and in the also trangenic *Move 36* (2002/04).[168] However, since 2004, in his *Rabbit Remix*

---

[167]   Kac quoted by Osthoff, "Object Lessons," 22.

[168]   Besides the São Paulo Biennial, *Move 36* was also exhibited in 2004 at the Gwangju biennale in Korea, and in 2005 in Paris at the Biche de Bere Gallery, Sept. 28-Oct. 26. About *Move 36* see also: Elena

on-going series, Kac employs the media reception and circulation of his work across space and time as a new material for art making, thus re-defying and enlarging the concept of network while remixing the archive.

Porno-Poetry Performances

In 1979, Brazil's military government, under the pressure of public opinion, gave amnesty to all those involved in "political crimes." Political exiles began to return home. As the tight censorship of the 1970s began to erode, so did the polarization between left and right which was characterized, during the period, by the symbol of Latin American liberation Che Guevara contrasted against the symbol of North American imperialism Coca-Cola. According to Zuenir Ventura, during the ten years following the declaration of the AI-5 (Fifth Institutional Act, signed in 1968) that closed Congress and suspended all political and constitutional rights, approximately 500 films, 450 plays, 200 books, dozens of radio programs and more than 500 song lyrics, along with a dozen soap opera episodes, were censored.[169]

The country's slow return to democracy in the 1980s was accompanied by a shift in the focus of critical theory, from an essentialist Marxism centered on the problematic of class antagonism and commodity production to a fresh interest in the formation of the subject—semiotics, psychoanalytical theory,

---

Rossi, ed., *Eduardo Kac: Move 36* (Paris : Filigranes Éditions, 2005) with essays by David Rosenberg, Frank Popper, Didier Ottinger, Linda Weintraub and Hugues Marchal. All of Kac's transgenic works up to and including *Move 36* are documented in Eduardo Kac, *Telepresence & Bio Art: Networking Humans, Rabbits, & Robots* (Ann Arbor: University of Michigan Press, 2005).

[169]   Zuenir Ventura, *1968 O Ano que Não Terminou* (Rio de Janeiro: Nova Fronteira, 1988), 285.

and Foucauldian notions of power—followed by a new understanding of democracy as a task, rather than a gift to be given or taken.[170] This self-critical examination of authoritarian and chauvinistic streaks among the intellectual, political, and urban middle class was marked by two bestselling books written by a journalist returning from a long exile in Sweden: Fernando Gabeira. His first book, *O Que É Isso Companheiro* (What Is This Comrade?) is the autobiographical story of a young intellectual who joins the urban guerrillas in Rio de Janeiro, planning and executing the kidnapping of the American ambassador Charles Elbrick, who is then exchanged for fifteen political prisoners. Not much later the police shot Gabeira in the back, and he was arrested while trying to flee. The wound healed in prison, and he was released in a similar exchange between political prisoners and a kidnapped ambassador, this time Germany's. Gabeira went into exile in Algeria and then Sweden, returning to Brazil under the political amnesty declared in 1979. Gabeira has since renounced violence, remaining a political activist in the new democratic regime by holding a seat in Congress for the Green party.[171] Gabeira's second book, *O Crepúsculo do Macho* (The Sunset of the Macho) exposed the inherent machismo and homophobia in the leftist movement and in Brazilian society.[172]

---

[170]   Judith Butler, Ernesto Laclau, and Slavoj Zizek, *Contingency, Hegemony, and Universality* (London: Verso, 2000). The authors discuss the false notion, developed since the 1980s, of an opposition between Marxist theory and Lacanian and deconstructive analysis of the formation of the subject.

[171]   Fernando Gabeira, *O Que É Isso Companheiro* [What Is This, Comrade?] (Rio de Janeiro: Codecri, 1979). The book became a film of the same title directed by Bruno Barreto in 1997. (Titled in the English version *Four Days in September,* it received an Oscar nomination).

[172]   Fernando Gabeira, *O Crepúsculo do Macho* [The Sunset of the Macho] (Rio de Janeiro: Codecri, 1980).

At that time, as a young university student in Rio de Janeiro, Kac studied foreign languages, philosophy, and semiotics while working as an artist and writer. The Poesia Pornô (Porno-Poetry) movement he founded in 1980 helped shape this political context by reclaiming the public space. Kac explained the movement: "The performances from 1980 to 82 had elements of scatology, surprise, humor, subversion, gags, and the mundane. In these poetic performances, the so-called vulgar or bad words become noble and positive. Scatological discourse and political discourse were one and the same and were manifested through cheerful orgiastic liberation."[173] Kac's group performed in public places, such as the beach in Ipanema and the Cinelândia central square, the heart of Rio's downtown bohemian life, where the group performed on Friday evenings for two years (1980–1982). With an emphasis on public participation, the porno-poets staged semantic displacements beginning with the word *pornography*. They transformed misogynist and homophobic labels into sexually liberating expressions in a process analogous to that undergone years later in the United States by the word *nigger,* as appropriated by rap culture, or the word *dyke,* as reclaimed by lesbians. Through humor, the group activated verbal transgressions that were first and foremost playful, as well as sexual, and ultimately political, in a polysemic celebration of life. They operated in the transgressive spirit of the poet Oswald de Andrade who in the 1920s proposed "the permanent transformation of taboo into totem."[174]

---

[173]   Eduardo Kac, in interview with the author, July 8, 1994, Chicago.

[174]   Oswald de Andrade, "Anthropophagite Manifesto," in *Art in Latin America,* ed. Dawn Ades (London: South Bank Centre, 1989), 310.

Kac called attention to the centrality of the body as a site for cultural inscription and transformation: "In my work in the early 1980s the body was everything. The body was the tool I used to question conventions, dogmas and taboos—patriarchy, religion, heterosexuality, politics, puritanism. The body became my writing medium ultimately."[175] In the artist's next phase of development, the role of the body and its relationship to language took an unprecedented turn.

Holopoetry: Meaning in Flux and the Viewer in Movement

Whereas Kac's porno-poetry performances questioned political and cultural hegemonies, their language was tied to the political process of the early 1980s as well as to a long literary tradition. Kac's interest in experimental poetry, along with his desire to create a new poetic language, led him to search for a new medium. He found it in holography, a medium that had never been explored for poetic expression. Kac was interested in holography's time base potential, which enabled exploration of the inherent instability and flux he perceived in language: "In many of my holograms, time flows back and forth, in non-linear ways. The holographic medium allows me to work with language floating in space and time, breaking down, melting and dissolving, and recombining itself to produce new meanings."[176] Suspending words in this immaterial space, Kac's holographic poems offered a new field for poetic exploration in an international language. His engagement with holography marked a rupture with the porno-poetry movement and began his exploration of emerging technologies as artistic and

---

[175]   Kac quoted in Simone Osthoff, "Object Lessons," *World Art*, no. 1 (1996): 18–23.

[176]   Ibid., 20.

epistemological practices with the potential of global reach. He coined the term *holopoetry* to describe the body of work he developed in this medium from 1983 to 1993.[177] As he pushed the tradition of visual poetry beyond the page and beyond three-dimensional physical space, Kac explored holography as a four-dimensional medium, performing reading and writing as a time-based, open-ended process.

Containing words and letters in flux, the meanings of Kac's holopoems are created by the viewers' movements and points of view, underscoring the direct relation between knowledge and positionality. As viewers read these images differently, depending on their relative position and movement in relation to the picture plane, these works suggest that location is an important category in signifying practices—in determining what we know, how, and why. Kac's holopoems give form to the dynamics he sees in language and communication processes. For him, meaning is always a process of negotiation that happens through dialogue and shared communication: "Nothing exists until you claim it, until you create your own narrative, until you construct it."[178] This belief drives his emphasis on the interactive and dialogical practices that underlie his telecommunications and telepresence events, which take these explorations into the global network.[179]

---

[177]   Eduardo Kac, "Holopoetry," *Visible Language* 30, no. 2 (1996): 184–212.

[178]   Kac quoted by Osthoff, "Object Lessons," 23.

[179]   Kac's emphasis on the idea of dialogue is based in part on the philosopher Martin Buber's (1878–1965) notion of relations of reciprocity and intersubjectivity between "I" and "Thou," and relations of objectification between "I" and "It," as well as on the Russian literary critic Mikhail Bakhtin's (1895–1975) discussion of the dialogical function of literature and language.

Text in the Network and the Network as Medium: Telecommunications and Telepresence Before the Web

Created and experienced digitally between 1985 and 1986, Kac's first works on the electronic network were videotexts.[180] He has stated that the early 1980s marked the culmination of the process of dematerialization of the art object and the beginning of the creation of immaterial (digital) art.[181] For him, two landmark events created the cultural conditions for this shift: the popularization of the personal computer and the rise of the global electronic network. Kac's early digital and telecommunication works emphasized process over product, giving form to communication exchanges that involved reciprocity and multidirectionality. Like his holopoems, Kac's videotexts continued to produce playful interrelations between

---

[180]   Kac's Web site <http://www.ekac.org> defines videotext as follows: The videotext system allows users to log on with a remote terminal and access sequences of pages through regular phone lines. This videotext network was a precursor to today's Internet and functioned very much like it, with sites containing information about countless subjects. It also allowed users to send messages to one another (email). Different countries, such as UK, France, Japan, Canada, USA and Brazil, implemented different versions of the videotext concept under their own names. The UK called it Prestel. The Brazilian system was dubbed Videotexto. In Canada it was known as Telidon. In the USA the network was named Videotex. Under the name "Minitel," France implemented a comprehensive videotext network that was widely used throughout the 1980s. In 1984 Minitel terminals were distributed to subscribers free of charge, which helped to further popularize the network. From 1983 to 1994 (the period of the Internet boom), use of the Minitel grew continuously. In 1995 there were 7 million Minitel terminals in France. Although most countries no longer use videotext, the medium is still employed in France. It is also possible to access the Minitel through the web.

[181]   Eduardo Kac, "Brasil High Tech, O cheque ao pós-moderno," *Folha de São Paulo,* April 16, 1986.

the activities of writing and reading, addressing a range of different subjects.

Tesão (1985/1986) is a videotext animated poem shown online and on site as part of the group exhibition Brasil High-Tech, realized in 1986, at the Galeria de Arte do Centro Empresarial Rio in Rio de Janeiro and organized by Kac and Flavio Ferraz. *Tesão* is a declaration of love to Ruth, whom Kac later married. The three-word sentence that formed this videotext spoke of love in terms of desire. The colorful letters formed slowly on the monitor in a continuous line diagram. After all the letters of the first word had completed their graphic choreography, the screen became blank, and new letters started to form the second word in a similarly symmetrical, cinematic rhythm. A third word was made of solid and colorful letters that overlapped and filled the screen. The letters displayed on the screen in symmetrical designs did not convey meaning as graphic forms in space, but as animations in time. As letters and words were formed in slow motion, viewers interpreted the fleeting configurations as if they were changing their meaning.

D/eu/s, from 1986, was a videotext-animated poem, also part of the Brasil High-Tech exhibition. It was a black and white bar code with numbers and letters on the bottom that appeared in a small area centered on the screen (the proportion of the image to the screen was that of a bar code to a product). When viewers logged on they first saw a black screen, followed by a small, white, centered rectangle. Slowly, vertical bars descended inside the horizontal rectangle. At the bottom, viewers saw apparently random letters and numbers, reminding them of conventional bar codes. Upon close scrutiny the viewer noticed that the letters formed the word *Deus* (God). The spacing of the letters revealed *eu* (I) inside *Deus*. The numbers also were not random but indicated the date when the work was produced and uploaded to the Brazilian videotext network. The date also offered a second reading: 64/86 brackets the years between the military coup in 1964 and the height of public demand for the return of democratic elections in the Diretas Já (Democratic Elections Now) movement, which also coincided with the forward-looking exhibition Brasil High-Tech. The multiple meanings this short poem created—between humans and God, between God and the commodity labeling/identity to be read by scanners, and between the public demand for democracy and the utopian promises of the global network (still national at the time)—would be reexamined by Kac years later in his 1997 biotelematic performance *Time Capsule* and in his transgenic work *Genesis* from 1999.[182]

Alongside videotexts, Kac's early work with telecommunications, networks, and telepresence that preceded the Web further emphasized dialogic processes occurring in real time. He employed slow-scan TV (a kind of video phone), fax-TV hybrids, and fax performances in process-based works in which the process itself brought certain kinds of meanings to the work, such as a cinematic sense of progression, sequencing, and transformations that included interruptions, delays, and the artist's interferences while images were still being received. These works from the mid- to the late 1980s include *Conversation* (slow-scan TV) and *Retrato Suposto–Rosto Roto* (Presumed Portrait–

Foul Face) (fax/TV hybrid).[183]

---

[182]   Peter T. Dobrila and Aleksandra Kostic, eds., *Eduardo Kac: Telepresence, Biotelematics, and Transgenic Art* (Kibla, Slovenia: Maribor, 2000).

[183]   Other related works not examined here are *Three City Link* (slow-scan TV), 1989; *Impromptu* (fax and slow-scan TV), 1990; *Interfaces* (slow-scan TV), 1990; *Elastic Fax 1* (fax), 1991; *Elastic Fax II* (fax), 1994; and *Dialogical Drawing* (telecommunication sculpture) 1994.

Conversation was a slow-scan TV event realized at the Centro Cultural Três Rios in São Paulo on November 17, 1987. The slow-scan TV allowed the transmission and reception of sequential still video images over regular phone lines. The images that comprised the piece each took from eight to twelve seconds to form. Instead of considering each picture as a cinematic representation, Kac explored the live process of image formation. This was also the principle of *Retrato Suposto–Rosto Roto* (1988), created in collaboration with Mario Ramiro, who at one end of this fax conversation operated a fax machine from a live TV program in São Paulo, while Kac, at the other end, carried out a visual fax dialogue from his studio, thus connecting private and public realms. (According to Kac, "The basis of this link was a real time operation utilizing the fax as a dialogic medium, in the context of a television broadcast, a unidirectional system of mass communication. The goal was not to create pictures remotely but to explore the interactive, improvisational quality of both personal and public telecommunications media simultaneously, integrating the apparently antagonist media into a single process."[184]

In 1984, Kac started to create telepresence or remote-presence events. These telepresence works mobilized dislocations between place and space, that is, between the work's *literal* site, such as a gallery installation, its *symbolic* or *rhetorical* place, such as the topos of Eden, and the virtual space of the electronic network. These experiences of dislocation between real and virtual spaces are more common than we think, Kac observed: "We have developed concepts about cultures that we have never seen, never experienced. In my telepresence installations, I'm making geographic displacements that reflect

---

[184]   Eduardo Kac, "Telearte em rede," *O Globo* (Segundo Caderno, Rio de Janeiro), September 4, 1988. See also <http://www.ekac.org/rostoroto.html>.

that."[185] This complex new geography in which telepresence art operates emphasizes real time over real space, enabling a remote perception of the world from the point of view of the other, of the object—through the scale/lenses/eyes of the telerobot, "in a non-metaphysical out-of-body experience, if you will."[186]

Kac's first telepresence project dates from 1984, it was never realized as a result of countless technical obstacles. Titled *Cyborg,* the project involved three different Rio de Janeiro galleries—Galleria Cândido Mendes, Funarte, and Escola de Artes Visuais do Parque Lage—and the remote control of sculptural-robotic objects. In 1986, Kac realized his first telepresence work, *RC Robot.* He worked with radio-controlled telerobotics in the context of the exhibition Brasil High-Tech. The artist used a seven-foot-tall anthropomorphic robot as a host who conversed with exhibition visitors in real time. The robot's voice was that of a human being transmitted via radio. Exhibition visitors did not see the telerobot operator, who was telepresent in the robot's body. Still in the context of the exhibition, the robot was used in a dialogical performance realized with Otavio Donasci, in which the robot interacted with Donasci's videocreature (a human performer with a TV monitor for a head). Through the robotic body, a human (hidden away) improvised responses to the videocreature's prerecorded utterances.

Between 1987 and 1988, still in Rio de Janeiro, Kac drew sketches of two small telerobots to be controlled by participants in two distant cities. The idea was to enable a participant in city A to control a telerobot in city B and vice versa. The ideas explored in these sketches would lay the groundwork for the *Ornitorrinco Project,* Kac's name for the

185   Kac quoted by Osthoff, "Object Lessons," 23.
186   Ibid., 22.

small telerobot he would create with Ed Bennett in Chicago in 1989 (*Ornitorrinco* in Portuguese means "platypus," which, as an egg-laying mammal, is a hybrid animal). The *Ornitorrinco Project* was developed until 1996, and became increasingly more complex, as Kac employed telecommunications to mediate relations among people, animals, plants, and robots. In his telepresence events, process is produced by all the forces, types of use, programs, glitches, and actions taken by participants, in a web of relationships that unfolds in real time.

Kac's emphasis on dialogue and two-way exchanges disregards essentialist

identities while exposing the fragility and fluidity of meaning. His poetic explorations of signifying practices, geographic dislocations, and multipositioned spectatorship examine processes of identity constitution and fragmentation. The activism of his early porno-poetry performances on the Ipanema beach informs the cultural and ethical responsibility that characterizes his critical attitude: "If we don't question how technology affects our lives, if we don't take charge, if we don't use these technological media to raise questions about contemporary life, who is going to do it?"[187]

---

[187]   Ibid., 23.

Rara Avis: Turning the Spectacular Into the Speculative

As part of his dialogic practice, Kac often forged new venues for his work, and thus approached art institutions less as a hardware and container of culture and more as an interface, where institutions might function as software, frame, or site— one more node of his ephemeral ecologies. For instance, when in 1996 Kac was invited by the Nexus Contemporary Art in Atlanta (now Atlanta Contemporary Art Center) as part of the cultural events surrounding the Olympic games, that first rate art venue only had telephone and fax machines. Kac brought the Internet to their galleries for the creation of the *Rara Avis* installation, which networked the Nexus Contemporary Art to the Internet through three protocols: CU-SeeMe, the Web, and the MBone [*Fig. 14*]. In this work local and remote participants experienced a large aviary from the point of view of a telerobotic macaw placed among thirty live birds.[188]

---

[188]   *Rara Avis* premiered as part of the exhibition Out of Bounds: New Work by Eight Southeast Artists, curated by Annette Carlozzi and Julia Fenton (Atlanta: Nexus Contemporary Art Center, June 28-August 24, 1996). In 1997, *Rara Avis* traveled to three other venues: The Jack Blanton Museum of Art, Austin, Texas; The Centro Cultural de Belém, Lisbon, Portugal; and the Casa de Cultura Mario Quintana, Porto Alegre, Brazil, as part of the *I Bienal de Artes Visuais do Mercosul.*

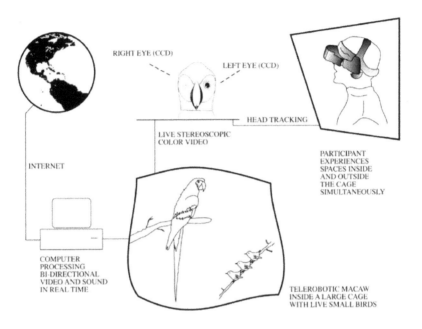

RIGHT EYE (CCD)

LEFT EYE (CCD)

HEAD TRACKING

LIVE STEREOSCOPIC
COLOR VIDEO

INTERNET

PARTICIPANT
EXPERIENCES
SPACES INSIDE
AND OUTSIDE
THE CAGE
SIMULTANEOUSLY

COMPUTER
PROCESSING
BI-DIRECTIONAL
VIDEO AND SOUND
IN REAL TIME

TELEROBOTIC MACAW
INSIDE A LARGE CAGE
WITH LIVE SMALL BIRDS

Figure 14. Eduardo Kac, *Rara Avis*, 1996. Diagram. The installation
included an aviary, a telerobot, thirty live zebra finches, and a VR
headset, connected to the Web and the M-bone. (Photo provided by the
artist)

The VR technology *Rara Avis* employed was state of
the art in 1996, and Kac used it to subvert common expectations
about immersive technologies. Instead of offering a simulation,
he turned the viewers' gaze back upon themselves by projecting
in real-time stereoscopic 3D color images of the viewers in the
gallery. The two cameras were located in the eyes of the exotic
robotic bird within the aviary. Gallery visitors wearing the VR

headset saw from close up the thirty live birds flying, eating, and perched on branches quite close to the camera lenses. They simultaneously saw themselves in the image background, standing outside the aviary wearing the VR headset, and thus being both inside and outside the aviary at the same time. Kac summed up this reversal: "In *Rara Avis*, the spectacular became specular, forcing the viewer to see himself or herself through the eye of the so-called exotic being."[189]

While denying users of VR technology the simulated worlds they normally expected, offering instead a reflective visual experience of simultaneously seeing and being seen, the artist in addition networked the headset images with remote participants on the Web. Participant-viewers elsewhere saw on their computer screens the same real-time video images projected inside the VR headset, and if they used their own home cameras and the CU-SeeMe program, they could also send live audiovisuals of themselves, thus seeing and talking to other users. Strange conversations took place. As a privileged viewer-participant of *Rara Avis* in three of its exhibition venues (I was present in the gallery in Atlanta in 1996, at the Mercosul Biennial in Porto Alegre, Brazil in 1997, and as a remote viewer-participant using CU-SeeMe during the opening of *Rara Avis* in Austin, Texas), I experienced firsthand not only the uncanny dislocation of point of view the work prompted viewers in the gallery to engage, but also how the Internet stratification and fluctuating traffic patterns produced alternative experiences of the work. During the opening of the exhibition in Texas, sounds and images were being exchanged in real time among remote participants combined with the voices and images of the viewers and birds in the Austin gallery. My remote reception of the sounds was not always synchronized with that of the images. Fluctuations and delays produced fragmented moving images

---

[189]   Kac, *Telepresence & Bio Art*, 163.

and disjointed real-time conversations, which at some point included the feedback of my own voice as a ghostly presence in the gallery opening night.

Time Capsule: Implanting the Digital Archive in the Artist's Body

Time Capsule was a more dramatic and controversial, yet equally bold network installation and performance. After being censored by the first venue where the event was schedule to take place—the Itaú Cultural in São Paulo[190]—another prestigious venue in the city merely one block away from the first—the cultural center Casa das Rosas—offered to showcase the performance and exhibition. The work consisted of a microchip implant, a live television broadcast and a simultaneous webcast of the performance, interactive telerobotic web-scanning of the implant, a remote database registration, and additional display elements, including seven sepia-toned photographs and X-rays of the artist's ankle before and after the implant *[Figs. 15, 16, 17]*.

---

[190]   Patricia Decia, "Bioarte: Eduardo Kac tem obra polêmica vetada no ICI," *Folha de São Paulo,* Ilustrada, (October 10, 1997), 13.

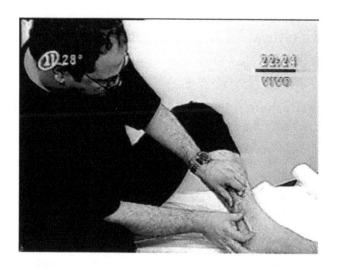

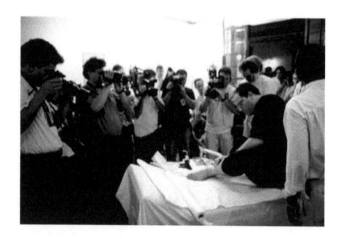

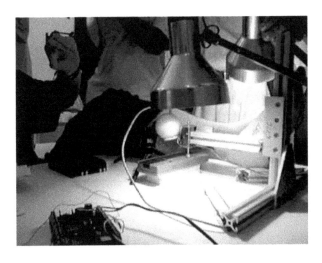

Figures 15, 16, 17. Eduardo Kac *Time Capsule,* 1997. Microchip implant, simulcast on TV and the Web, remote scanning of the microchip through the Internet, photographs, X-Ray. (Photo provided by the artist)

The performance-media-spectacle took place on November 11, 1997, when the artist implanted a memory chip in his own ankle in a gallery exhibition that displayed old sepia family photographs on the wall (the only images that survived after his family had to flee Poland in 1939), thus bringing to the critical forefront of his work questions of information, documentation and history, which have always been connected in Kac's artistic practice from the beginning of his career. Many journalists with cameras of all sizes filled the gallery documenting the microchip bio-implant simultaneously in the print media, in a live broadcast on TV, through later TV broadcast updates, and on the Web. After the insertion of the microchip in the artist's body the digital information it contained was remotely retrieved by a scanner attached to a computer, as

the artist registered the chip's ID number over the Internet in a
databank in the U.S.

Time Capsule locates a digital archive—a computer
memory unit used to track animals—inside the artist's body
underlying the increasing embodiment of technology: "Scanning
of the implant remotely via the Web revealed how the
connective tissue of the global digital network renders obsolete
the skin as a protective boundary demarcating the limits of the
body."[191] In addition, Time Capsule occupied many sites
simultaneously: the artist's body, the gallery space, the mass
media and the Web, as this memory archive traversed the skin
boundary and thus blurred its inside/outside limits.

Rabbit Remix: The News Media Archive as Medium for Art Making

The media, understood both as the plural of medium,
and as the means of mass communication (such as newspapers,
magazines, radio, and television), has been explored as a
medium by the artist since the beginning of his career. Yet,
throughout the twentieth century, aside from a few revolutionary
and enthusiastic moments such as the one led by the Russian
Constructivists between 1917-25 and by the Bauhaus artists
between 1919-1933, in general the relationship between the
avant-gardes and the mass media remained controversial.
Examples include Pablo Picasso Cubist's collages of 1912;
Orson Welles' famous adaptation of the sci-fi novel War of the
Worlds in a radio broadcast on the day prior to Halloween in
1938; Jackson Pollock's 1949 photo spread on the pages of Life
magazine; and Andy Warhol's profitable engagement with
celebrity and commodity culture in the 1960s.

---

[191]   Kac, Telepresence & Bio Art, 232.

Throughout the 1970s and in many parts of the world, video art began to further close this gap as visual artists increasingly embraced video as an experimental time-based medium. Nam June Paik's *Global Groove* 1973 anticipated the MTV aesthetics and Martha Rosler's 1975 deadpan performance of domesticity in *Semiotics of the Kitchen* contrasts sharply with the visual exuberance of Mariko Mori's high-tech nirvana-pop videos of the 1990s, as well as with Mathew Barney's ambitious epic *Cremaster Cycle* completed in 2002. Over the last fifteen years, artists such as Orlan and Stelarc have in different ways been highly skilled in framing their notorious performances as public media spectacles. Others, such as Andrea Zittel, have collapsed the boundaries between art and design by creating their own brand of products. And because of the early media acclaim she received, Cindy Sherman has had to negotiate her media image as another dimension of her identity and numerous self-portraits throughout her career.

Nevertheless, Kac's performance is uncommon among artists and theorists because he is fluent in multiple languages and fields of knowledge, ultimately influencing the history of new media as well as participating in the theoretical discussion his work generates. Besides being an accomplished researcher and writer Kac has always articulated the experience of creative work with aesthetic theory. Among the few artists who can lucidly speak about aesthetic concepts in relation to other disciplines such as science, technology, and poetry, his voice debunks the fantasy that studio work does not involve either theory or research, thus grounding his creations both in experiment and debate. Always minding the cognitive structures of communication processes, Kac's networks and writings continuously connect art and life, culture and nature, art writing and art making.

Besides being the title of his Rio de Janeiro solo show in 2004, *Rabbit Remix* also titles an on-going series of works that have three phases: the first was the creation of the *GFP*

Bunny in 2000; the second was the *Free Alba!* campaign, carried
out by the artist in 2001-02; and the third is his on-going
orchestration of the ensuing global media response to this work
[*Figs. 6-11*]. The *Rabbit Remix* series extends the discussion of
bio art in relation to science, ethics, religion, and culture, which
Kac continues to address beyond the space of the gallery in
many forms such as mass-media articles and interviews,
academic books and essays, lectures and debates, as well as
public interventions, examined in chapter one. [192]

While artist's writings usually explore conceptual and
creative processes, increasingly artists have to fill the gap left by
art criticism.[193] Formerly, artists' writings were included within
the discourses of art history as source material, but not as
authoritative voices. Nevertheless, they continue to disrupt these

---

[192]   Further editorial projects by Kac are: Eduardo Kac, ed., *Signs
of Life: Bio Art and Beyond* (Cambridge: MIT Press, 2006); and
Eduardo Kac, ed., *Media Poetry: An International Anthology* (Bristol:
Intellect, 2007), first published as a special issue of the journal *Visible
Language*, Vol. 30, N. 2., 1996.

[193]   The combination of art practice with critical research and
writing is about to become even more common in the United States
over the next decades because of the upcoming Ph.D. degree in studio
art. The question of what constitutes research in fine arts studio
education and the role of academic writing in such pursuit is open for
debate while it also points to new connections to be explored among
previously unrelated academic fields. See the multiple contributions to
this discussion by prominent artists and historians in "Art Schools: A
Group Crit," *Art in America*, May 2007, pp. 99-109. Further examples
of accomplished artists who are also critical writers in the U.S. include:
Donald Judd, *Complete Writings 1959–1975* (Press of the Nova Scotia
College of Art and Design, 2005); Andrea Fraser, *Museum Highlights:
The Writings of Andrea Fraser* (Cambridge, MA: MIT Press, 2005);
Martha Rosler, *Decoys and Disruptions: Selected Writings, 1975–2001*
(Cambridge, MA: MIT Press, 2004); Robert Smithson, *The Collected
Writings*, ed. Jack Flam (Berkeley: University of California Press,
1996); and Joseph Kosuth, *Art after Philosophy and After: Collected
Writings, 1996–1990* (Cambridge, MA: MIT Press, 1991).

discourses from within. From Marcel Duchamp's *Fountain* to Kac's *GFP Bunny*—revolutionary artistic practice often exposes art history's taboos, biases, and ideological frames. Kac's networks examine how technology-mediated environments structure our perception and cognition. By approaching networks as a medium and trope, that is by displacing visual perception and the clear location of voice and vision through viewer participation and interpolation in his networks (in which I include the effects produced by the artist's own voice and discursive body of work), Kac places aesthetic experience at the center of philosophical concerns, as a few philosophers have also done, among them Kant, Adorno, and Rancière. Kac's networks change the hierarchies and the function of institutions and the clear location of voice and vision among network participants, ultimately including our cognitive understanding of the "natural" within the environment of art.

Conclusion

The past is never dead. In fact, it's not even past.
William Faulkner

Despite the growing instability of the archive produced by the seamless flux between art and documentation, fiction and non-fiction, news media and history, we increasingly believe that everything should and could be safely stored and documented. Our need for constant computer memory upgrades confirms this hyper-archiving tendency. *Google* encourages our fantasy for an oracle that can answer any question and access any text, image, or sound. Online social networks promise constant connection with hundreds of friends from our past and present, not to mention the perfect date. Our fantasy of mastery over representation makes the media motto expressed by the *New York Times* since 1896 — "All the news that's fit to print" — also applicable to our archival illusions.[194]

And yet, we cannot freeze time nor document everything. It takes twenty-four hours to re-live twenty-four hours — and all we have is different media and perspectives. The more we document, the more information we produce, the less time we have to analyze it, and the further we are from where we started. Art and history increasingly connected in real time also share this paradox. And despite the growing access to recording devices and widespread information technology, we still cannot re-live or store experience, even if we can clone

---

[194]   About the changing attitudes towards newspaper archives and the policies that terminated them in favor of microfilmed records, please see Nicholson Baker's heroic research for the book *Double Fold: Libraries and the Assault on Paper* (2002), in which he examines the consequences in our collective memory caused by the uncritical use of "progressive" technologies that continuously shape our culture.

living beings or approach events phenomenologically. Increasingly inadequate is the way we usually represent time and space in our common experience: we place ourselves in the present with the past behind and the future ahead — a linear sequence, that can hardly address the temporal and spatial displacement produced by telecommunications technology, which is closer to the way our memory works, with gaps, faint records, repetitions, blind spots, flashbacks, imaginative jumps, associations, and daydreaming.

The impossibility of asserting the boundaries between art and documentation, fiction and non-fiction contributes to the epistemological crisis of not trusting one's own eyes. In order to understand many works of visual arts, being "blind" may be a required first step. Yet this often invisible and fluid dimension of the visual arts increasingly haunts critics and historians by positioning research on uncertain ground with methodological difficulties that cannot address what remains unresolved, often hidden and incalculable. This is a History in distress, struggling to move away from the enervating realm of infinite possibilities that frustrates our need for closure.

The current crisis of criticism suggests that the traditional methodologies of art history, theory and criticism — formal analysis, iconography, biography and autobiography, psychology, social history, and structuralism — largely based upon notions of mimetic representation and chronology, are increasingly incapable of addressing technical images and multimedia art practices, especially those involving media communications, science and technology. There is much in the visual arts that is non-visual, and Vilém Flusser's image theory is particularly relevant, precisely because of its iconoclastic and post-historical perspective. Fiction, as Flusser reminded us, has different meanings in different realms of knowledge. In literature, fiction is positive while in history it is negative and equated with illusion, false ideology, semblance, and mask. But fiction can also be understood as a scientific model, a hypothesis that helps designers and researchers approach reality. And it is perhaps this third meaning of fiction as a model of visualization and techno-imagination that can be the most productive for contemporary art theory and criticism.[195]

Therefore, art, literature and poetry are perhaps better positioned to navigate the anxiety of uncertainty and timelessness. They have often revealed history's blind spots by emphasizing the opacity of language and the complex relations between knowledge and the somatic body, which artists like Hélio Oiticica and cultural critics such as Avital Ronell insist upon by asking: Where does the body belong in the textual experience? What is the status of a reverie in thought? [196] In the effort to represent and stabilize past events, which ghosts does the archive have to avoid and evade, preserve or defend against? Beyond humidity, mold and insects, what other entropic forces oppose the process of archivization? What cannot be documented? Which memories can be materialized in form and space? Whose memories get to be preserved in archives? What kind of documental collection is formed when the artist is the archivist?

The reflections of Derrida's *Archive Fever* (1993) about origins and their bearing upon the archive's limits, taxonomy and logic were also the focus of José Saramago's novel *Todos os Nomes* (1997) [*All the Names*, 1999]. Saramago's novel explores the possibility of the break into the archive and the consequent

---

[195]   See Vilém Flusser "Da Ficção," in *Da Religiosidade: A Literatura e o Senso de Realidade* (São Paulo: Escrituras, 2002) [1967]; and also Gustavo Bernardo "Ciência e Ficção" in *Vilém Flusser, uma introdução*, Gustavo Bernardo, Anke Finger and Rainer Guldin, Eds. (São Paulo: Annablume, 2008).

[196]   Such questions along with the place of unknowability and invisibility in face of the hermeneutic compulsion to smooth over the disruption and the crisis of understanding are explored by Avital Ronell, in among other books, *Stupidity* (Chicago: University of Illinois Press, 2003).

break-down of its order. The novel takes place in the oldest and
most reliable archive in Lisbon — the site of a pre-modern
labyrinth-like structure, a depository of documents of births and
deaths that guarantees identity, as well as the clear boundary
between the archives of the living and of the dead. Saramago's
anti-hero José and the artist Eduardo Kac are exemplary
instances of archival disruption. How does one bring what is
outside into the inside? While José did so because of love and
reverie, Kac privileged communication and translation.
Beginning with poetry performances, the artist's exploration of
language and communications unfolded from *Holopoetry* to
Telepresence and Bio art. In his installation *Genesis* from 1999,
for instance, Kac translated a sentence from the *Bible*, from
English into Morse code and from that binary system into the
DNA protein of a bacteria, thus encoding language into a living
being, the metaphysical into the physical. Today, he continues to
produce new life forms — living artworks that destabilize
traditional boundaries between subjects and objects, the living
and the dead. The artist continuously connects the mythical
realm of religion with the science lab, the news media, the
gallery and the museum as well as the archive with all
institutions as nodes of his complex networks.

In contrast to the emergence of the modernist avant-
gardes who entered the twentieth century with a humanist
visionary bravado, and fought often violently, both aesthetically
and politically to bring about twin revolutions, avant-garde
artists entered the twenty-first century embracing uncertainty
and non-linear experiences, while raising questions about what it
means to be human. And if the historical avant-gardes
established a new departure in terms of inception, insemination,
and action, contemporary art is perhaps immersed in the scene of
arrival — how do we artists, critics and historians enter and
negotiate the economy of desire, technology, and capital, no
longer in terms of an utopian future but of an ever expanding
uncertain present? Do performances of the archive escape time

or promote an immersion in it? How do we historicize contemporary art when the archive is a database with generative potential?

For a visual artist, the distinction between interior and exterior is frequently dependent on the notion of surface, which can also ensure the perception of depth. Artists, such as Lygia Clark, often pointed out that the surface rather than superficial is where all power and content resides. For Clark, surface and depth, interior and exterior were but a continuum, which she first explored by removing the frame around the artwork and seamlessly connecting the space of representation and the architecture of the room around it. Through the topology of the Mobiüs Band, she connected inside and outside. She later explored surface in relation to blindness by creating masks that covered the eyes and encouraged seeing through other senses, especially touch. Clark and Oiticica suggested that our eyes need to see by other means and senses. They need to explore other visions and visualizations.

Today, information culture is at the same time widespread and invisible. It is ever more influential because of its unseen dimensions, this is also true in contemporary art with genetic engineering and nanotechnology becoming media for art making. The invisible scope of information technology and digital archives echo the phantasmagorical dimensions of images and imagination, particularly prominent in the second half of the nineteenth century, when alongside the development of photography and film, spiritualist circles and parapsychologists mobilized the imagination of many by producing apparitions and guaranteeing contacts with the dead. What remains constant in face of technological change is the archive's haunted dimensions, delusional fantasies and psychotic symptoms.

What happens then to history and criticism when along with the archive they become part of the artist's production tools? By participating in art's complex relays as media, often in real time, history, theory and criticism must engage documentation and memory with all its haunted and uncertain dimensions, prospective and retrospective perspectives, along with unexpected precedents and unlike predecessors. And even though the archive *mise-en-abyme* erodes the archive's former function and stability as a deposit of records and documents, it isn't a complete simulation masking an original and more authentic experience. The archive placed into infinity positions history and theory in a contingent, dynamic relation to art — without foundations. Consequently, either critics, historians and theorists engage as participants in art's complex relays by finding our place in it, or the artworks won't matter much.

During the process of writing this book, my own critical performance changed from that of a cultural translator, an art critic and historian who made complex artworks more docile in terms of archival possibilities, towards the exploration of more ex-centric points of view that acknowledge the excess that escapes understanding. Increasingly, the connections among the works I explored raised methodological questions without answers. In the process, I realized what the poet knows so well and the historian tries to bring to a standstill: that "the past is never dead. In fact, it's not even past."[197] As I conclude this book, I underline the haunting dimensions of the archive that escape, are invisible to, or disrupt representation. They also urge more contingent and dynamic histories in flux, often in real time, unsystematic and generative. The artists and theorists examined in these chapters created rich experiences that are sill unfolding and reverberating. I hope this examination of their original and unique performances in relation to the archive's changing ontology will contribute to foster other comparable critical and experimental histories.

---

[197]   William Faulkner, *Requiem for a Nun*, Act 1, Sc 3, 1951.

PRIMARY SOURCES

Archives

Lygia Clark archive, Rio de Janeiro, Brazil.
Hélio Oiticica archive, Rio de Janeiro, Brazil.
Vilém Flusser archive, Universität der Künste, Berlin, Germany.
Paulo Bruscky archive, Recife, Brazil.
Eduardo Kac archive, Oak Park, USA.

Interviews

Osthoff, Simone. Unpublished interview with Paulo Bruscky on September 23, 2004 at the Parque Ibirapuera, São Paulo Bienal.
Osthoff, Simone. *Eduardo Kac: a Conversation with the Artist. Art.es*, International Contemporary Art, No. 23, Madrid, Spain, Dec. 2007: 74-79.

Letters and Newspaper Articles

Clark, Lygia and Hélio Oiticica. *Cartas 1964-1974.* Luciano Figueiredo, org. Rio de   Janeiro: Editora,   UFRJ, 1996.
Decia, Patricia. "Bioarte: Eduardo Kac tem obra polêmica vetada no ICI." *Folha de São Paulo,* October 10, 1997, Ilustrada.
Gewen, Barry. "State of the Art," *New York Times*, December 11, 2005.
Harwood, William. "Um vôo em que tudo deu certo." *Jornal do Comércio,* April 3, 1992, Ciência/Meio Ambiente, Recife, Brazil.
Kac, Eduardo. "Brasil High Tech, O cheque ao pós-moderno." *Folha de São Paulo,* April 16, 1986.
Kac, Eduardo. "Telearte em rede." *O Globo.* September 4, 1988, Segundo Caderno. Rio de Janeiro, Brazil.

Lubow, Arthur. "After Frida," *The New York Times Magazine* March 23, 2008. 54-61.

DVDs and CDs

Art : 21—Art in the Twenty-First Century. Season 4. 220 min. PBS Home Video, 2007.

Byrne, David. *E. E. E. I.: Envisioning Emotional Epistemological Information.* Steidl and Pace/MacGill, Göttingen, Germany 2003.

Fiennes, Sophie and Slavoj Zizek. *The Pervert's Guide to the Cinema.* A Lone Star, Mischief Films, Amoeba Film, 2006.

Kofman, Amy Ziering and Kirby Dick, *Derrida.* Zeitgeist Video, 2003.

Manovich, Lev and Andreas Kratky. *Soft Cinema: Navigating the Database*, MIT Press, 2005.

Quays Brothers. *Phantom Museums: The Short Films of the Quay Brothers.* Zeitgeist Films, 2007.

Taylor, Astra. *Zizek!.* Zeitgeist Video, 2005.

SECONDARY SOURCES

"Art Schools: A Group Crit." *Art in America.* May 2007: 99-109.

Ades, Dawn. *Art in Latin America: The Modern Era, 1820-1980.* New Haven, CT: Yale University Press, 1989.

Adorno, Theodore W. *Aesthetic Theory.* Robert Hullot-Kentor, trans. Minneapolis: University of Minnesota Press, 1997.

Adorno, Theodore, and Max Horkheimer. *Dialética do Esclarecimento.* Rio de Janeiro: Jorge Zahar Editores, 1944.

Agamben, Giorgio. *Homo Sacer, Sovereign Power and Bare Life*. Daniel Heller-Roazen, trans. Stanford, California: Stanford University Press, 1998.

_____. *The Open: Man and Animal*. Kevin Attell, trans. Stanford, California: Stanford University Press, 1998.

Aguilar, Gonzalo. *Poesia Concreta Brasileira*. São Paulo: EDUSP, 2005.

Amaral, Aracy. *Projeto Construtivo Brasileiro na Arte (1950-1962)*. São Paulo: Mec-Funarte, Secretaria da Cultura, Ciencia e Tecnologia do Estado de São Paulo, 1977.

_____. *Arte e Meio Artístico: Entre a Feijoada e o X-Burger*. São Paulo: Nobel, 1982.

_____. *Arte Pra Quê? A Preocupação Social na Arte Brasileira, 1930-1970*. São Paulo: Nobel, 1984.

Amaral, Aracy and Paulo Herkenhoff. *Ultramodern: The Art of Contemporary Brazil*. Washington, DC: National Museum of Women in the Arts, 1993.

Andrade, Oswald de. "Anthropophagite Manifesto." in *Art in Latin America*. Dawn Ades, ed. New Haven: Yale University Press, 1989.

Arantes, Otilia Beatriz Fiori. "Depois das Vanguardas." *Arte em Revista #7*. August 1983.

Augé, Marc. *Non-Places: Introduction to an Anthropology of Supermodernity*. John Howe, trans. New York: Verso, 1995.

_____. *An Anthropology for Contemporaneous Worlds*. Amy Jacobs, trans. Stanford, California: University of Stanford Press, 1999.

Badiou, Alain. *Handbook of Inaesthetics*. Alberto Toscano, trans. Stanford, California: Stanford University Press, 2005.

_____. *The Century*. Alberto Toscano, trans. Malden, MA: Polity Press, 2005.

Baker, Nicholson. *Double Fold: Libraries and the Assault on Paper*. New York: Vintage Books, 2002.

Bakhtin, Mikhail R. *The Dialogic Imagination*. Caryl Emerson and Michael Holquist, trans. Austin, TX: University of Texas Press, 1981.

_____. *Art and Answerability: Early Philosophical Essays.* Austin, TX: University of Texas Press, 1990.

Basbaum, Ricardo and Paulo Reis and Ricardo Resende, eds. *Panaroma da Arte Brasileira 2001.* São Paulo: Museu de Arte Moderna de São Paulo, 2001.

_____. *Arte Contemporânea Brasileira.* Rio de Janeiro: Contra Capa, 2001.

Basualdo, Carlos and Nelson Aguilar. "Visible Means of Support." *Art Forum.* September 1994.

Basualdo, Carlos, ed. *Tropicália: a Revolution in Brazilian Culture.* Chicago: Museum of Contemporary Art of Chicago, 2005.

_____, org. *Hélio Oiticica, Quasi-Cinemas.* Ohio and New York: The Wexler Art Center and the New Museum of Contemporary Art, 2001.

Baudrillard, Jean. *Simulacra and Simulation.* Sheila Faria Glaser, trans. Ann Arbor: University of Michigan Press, 1995.

_____. *The Conspiracy of Art.* Ames Hodges, trans. New York and Los Angeles: Semiotext(e), 2005.

Benjamin, Walter. *Illuminations.* Hanna Harendt, ed. New York: Schocken Books, 1969.

_____. *The Arcades Project.* Howard Eiland and Kevin MacLaughlin, trans. Cambridge, MA and London: The Belknap Press of Harvard University Press, 1999.

Bernardo, Gustavo, Anke Finger, and Rainer Guldin. *Vilém Flusser: Uma Introdução.* São Paulo: AnnaBlume, 2008.

Biennial Brazil Século XX. São Paulo: Fundação Biennial de São Paulo, 1994.

Bill, Max. "The Mathematical Way of Thinking in the Visual Art of Our Time." In *The Visual Mind: Art and Mathematics,* edited by Michele Emmer. Cambridge: MIT Press, 1993. Originally published in *Werk 3,* 1949.

Bishop, Claire, ed. *Participation.* Documents of Contemporary Art Series. London: Whitechapel; and Cambridge, MA: MIT Press, 2006.

Bois, Yve-Alain and Rosalind Krauss. *Formless, a User's Guide.* New York: Zone Books, 1997.

Borges, Jorge Luis. *Labyrinths*. New York: New Directions Books, 1964.

Borja-Villel, Manuel J. and Nuria Enguita Mayo and Luciano Figueiredo, eds. *Lygia Clark*. Barcelona: Fundació Antoni Tàpies, 1998.

Bourriaud, Nicolas. *Relational Aesthetics*. Simon Pleasance and Fronza Woods, trans. France: les presses du reel, 2002.

Brett, Guy. *Kinetic Art*. London: Studio-Vista, 1968.

_____. "A Radical Leap." In *Art in Latin America: The Modern Era, 1820-1980*. Dawn Ades, ed. New Haven, CT: Yale University Press, 1989.

_____. "Hélio Oiticica: Reverie and revolt." *Art in America*. January 1989.

_____. "Lygia Clark: In Search of the Body." *Art in America*. July 1994.

_____. "A Paradox of Containment." *Witte de With Cahier* #2, 1994.

_____. *Brasil Experimental*. Rio de Janeiro: Contra Capa, 2005.

Brett, Guy, Catherine David, Chris Dercon, Luciano Figueiredo and Lygia Pape, eds. *Hélio Oiticica*. Minneapolis, MN: Walker Art Center; and Rotterdam: Witte de With Center for Contemporary Art, 1993.

Brito, Ronaldo. *A Experiência Crítica*. São Paulo: Cosacnaify, 2005.

Brito, Ronaldo. *Neoconcretismo*. Rio de Janeiro: Funarte/Instituto Nacional de Artes Plásticas, 1985.

Britton, Sheilah and Dan Collins, eds. *The Eighth Day: The Transgenic Art of Eduardo Kac*. Tempe: Arizona State University, 2003.

Bürger, Peter. *Theory of the Avant-Garde*. Michael Shaw, trans. Minneapolis: The University of Minnesota Press, 2004.

Cage, John. *Empty Words, Writings '73-'78*. Middletown, CT: Wesleyan University Press, 1973.

_____. *John Cage: An Anthology*. Richard Kostelanetz, ed. New York: Da Capo Press, 1991.

Camnitzer, Luis, et al, eds. *Global Conceptualism: Points of Origin, 1950s-1980s*. New York: Queens Museum of Art, 1999.

Canongia, Ligia. *Quase Cinema*. Rio de Janeiro: Funarte, 1981.

Cardoso, Rafael, org. *O Design Brasileiro Antes do Design*. São Paulo: Cosacnaify, 2005.

Carlozzi, Annette, and Julia Fenton. *Out of Bounds: New Work by Eight Southeast Artists*. Atlanta, Georgia: Nexus Contemporary Art Center, 1996.

Carnevale, Fulvia and John Kelsey in conversation with Jacques Rancière. "Art of the Possible." *Art Forum*. March 2007: 256-259.

Carvajal, Rina and Alma Ruiz, eds. *The Experimental Exercise of Freedom* Los Angeles: MOCA, 1999.

Castro, Ruy. *O Anjo Pornográfico*. Rio de Janeiro: Companhia das Letras, 1992.

Chandler, Annmarie and Norie Neumark, eds. *At a Distance: Precurssors to Art and Activism on the Internet*. Cambridge, MA: MIT Press, 2005.

Chomsky, Noam and Edward S. Herman. *Manufacturing Consent*. Pantheon Books, 1988.

Cixous, Hélene. "Introduction." *The Stream of Life*. Clarice Lispector. Verena Conley, trans. Minneapolis: University of Minnesota Press, 1989.

_____. *The Hélène Cixous Reader*. Susan Sellers, ed. London: Routlege, 1994.

_____. *Three Steps on the Ladder of Writing*. New York: Columbia University Press, 1993.

Clark, Lygia, et al. "The Neo-concretist Manifesto." *October the Second Decade, 1986-1996*. Cambridge, MA: MIT Press, 1997.

Clark, Lygia. *Lygia Clark*. Rio de Janeiro: Funarte, 1980.

Clark, T.J. *Farewell to an Idea: Episodes From a History of Modernism*. New Haven, CT: Yale University Press, 2001.

Clarke, Bruce and Linda Dalrymple Henderson, eds. *From Energy to Information: Representation in Science and Technology, Art and Literature*. Stanford, California: The University of Stanford Press, 2002.

Clifford, James. *The Predicament of Culture*. Cambridge: Harvard University Press, 1988.

Cocchiarale, Fernando, and Anna Bella Geiger. *Abstracionismo Geométrico e Informal.* Coleção Temas e Debates #5. Rio de Janeiro: Funarte, 1987.

Coles, Alex, ed. *Design and Art.* Documents of Contemporary Art Series. Cambridge, MA: MIT Press, 2007.

Coutinho, Wilson and Cristina Aragão. *Opinião 65/30 anos.* Rio de Janeiro: Centro Cultural Banco do Brasil, 1995.

Cosentino, Donald, ed. *Sacred Arts of Haitian Vodou.* Los Angeles, California: UCLA Fowler Museum, 1995.

Cubitt, Sean. *Cinema Effect.* Cambridge, MA: MIT Press, 2004.

DaMatta, Roberto. *Carnaval, Malandros e Heróis.* Rio de Janeiro: Editora Guanabara, 1990.

David, Catherine. "The Great Labyrinth." In *Hélio Oiticica.* Catherine David et all, org. Minneapolis: The Walker Art Center, 1993.

Debord, Guy. *The Society of the Spectacle.* New York: Zone Books, 1995.

Deleuze, Gilles. *Cinema 1: The Movement-Image.* Minneapolis: The University of Minnesota Press, 1986.

_____. *Cinema 2: The Time-Image.* Minneapolis: The University of Minnesota Press, 1989.

_____. *The Fold: Leibniz and the Baroque.* Tom Conley, trans. Minneapolis: The University of Minnesota Press, 1993.

Deleuze, Gilles and Félix Guattari. *A Thousand Plateaus: Capitalism and Schizophrenia.* Brian Massumi, trans. Minneapolis: University of Minnesota Press, 1987.

_____. *Anti-Oedipus.* Minneapolis: The University of Minnesota Press, 1983.

_____. *What is Philosophy?* New York: Columbia University Press, 1991.

Dely, Carole. "Jacques Derrida: The *Perchance* of a Coming of the Otherwoman, the Deconstruction of 'Phallogocentrism' from Duel to Duo." *Sens [Public],* International Web Journal. (Oct.2007).

Derrida, Jacques. *Of Grammatology.* Gayatri Chakravorty Spivak, trans. Baltimore and London: Johns Hopkins University Press, 1997.

_____. *Writing and Difference.* Alan Bass, trans. Chicago: The University of Chicago Press, 1978.

_____. *Truth in Painting*. Geoffrey Bennington, trans. Chicago: The University of Chicago Press, 1987.

_____. *Memoirs of the Blind: The Self-Portrait and Other Ruins*. Pascale-Anne Brault, trans. Chicago: The University of Chicago Press, 1993.

_____. *The Gift of Death*. David Wills, trans. Chicago and London: The University of Chicago Press, 1995.

_____. *Archive Fever: a Freudian Impression*. Eric Prenowitz, trans. Chicago: The University of Chicago Press, 1996.

_____. *On Touching: Jean-Luc Nancy*. Christine Irizarry, trans. Stanford, California: Stanford University Press, 2005.

Derrida, Jacques, and Maurizio Ferraris. *A Taste for the Secret*. Cambridge, UK: Polity Press, 2001.

Dobrila, Peter T. and Aleksandra Kostic, eds. *Eduardo Kac: Telepresence, Biotelematics, and Transgenic Art*. Kibla, Slovenia: Maribor, 2000.

Duve, Thierry De. *Kant After Duchamp*. Cambridge, MA: MIT Press, 1996.

Eco, Humberto. *The Open Work*. Cambridge, MA: Harvard University Press, 1989.

_____. *Travels in Hyperreality*. Fort Washington, PA: Harvest Books 1990.

Elkins, James. *What Happened to Art Criticism*. Chicago: Prickly Paradigm Press, 2003.

_____. *Visual Studies: a Skeptical Introduction*. New York and London: Routledge, 2003.

_____, ed. *Is Art History Global?* The Art Seminar Series Vol. III. New York and London: Routledge, 2007.

____, ed. *The State of Art Criticism*. The Art Seminar Series Vol. IV. New York and London: Routledge, 2007.

Emmer, Michele, ed. *The Visual Mind: Art and Mathematics*. Cambridge: MIT Press, 1993.

Farias, Agnaldo. "Brief Guide to a Complex Panorama: Contemporary Art Production (1980 to 1994)." In *Biennial Brazil Século XX*. São Paulo: Fundação Biennial de São Paulo, 1994.

Favaretto, Celso. *A Invenção de Hélio Oiticica*. Texto e Arte #6. São Paulo: Edusp, 1992.

Fernandez, Maria. "Postcolonial Media Theory," *Art Journal* 58, no.3. (1999): 58-73.

Figueiredo, Luciano. "The Other Malady." *Third Text*. 28/29. Autumn/Winter 1994.

Flusser, Vilém. *Natural:mente: vários acessos ao significado da natureza*. São Paulo: Duas Cidades, 1978.

_____. *Ficções Filosóficas*. São Paulo: EDUSP, 1998.

_____. *A Dúvida*. Rio de Janeiro: Relume Dumará, 1999.

_____. *The Shape of Things: A Philosophy of Design*. London, UK: Reaktion Books, 1999.

_____. *Towards a Philosophy of Photography*. London, UK: Reaktion Books, 2000.

_____. *Da Religiosidade: A Literatura e o Senso de Realidade*. São Paulo: Escrituras, 2002.

_____. *Filosofia da Caixa Preta*. Rio de Janeiro: Relume Dumará, 2002.

_____. *Língua e Realidade*. São Paulo: Annablume, 2004.

_____. *A História do Diabo*. São Paulo: Annablume, 2005.

_____. *O Mundo Codificado*. Rafael Cardoso, org. São Paulo: Cosacnaify, 2007.

_____. *Bodenlos: Uma Autobiografia Filosófica*. São Paulo: Annablume, 2007.

Foster, Hal. *The Anti-Aesthetic*. Seattle: Bay Press, 1983.

_____, ed. *Vision and Visuality*. New York: Dia Art Foundation, 1988.

_____. *The Return of the Real: The Avant-Garde at the End of the Century*, Cambridge, MA: MIT Press, 1996.

_____. *Design and Crime (and other diatribes)*. New York and London: Verso, 2002.

Foster, Hal, et al. *Art Since 1900: Modernism, Antimodernism, Postmodernism*. Thames & Hudson, 2004.

Foucault, Michel. *A Arqueologia do Saber*. Luiz Felipe Baeta Neves, trans. Lisbon, Portugal and Petrópolis, Brazil: Editora Vozes, 1972.

_____. *A Verdade e as Formas Jurídicas*. Rio de Janeiro: Pontifícia Universidade Católica, 1974.

_____. *As Palavras e as Coisas*. Lisboa: Portugália Editora, 1966.

Francastel, Pierre. *Art & Technology in the Nineteenth and Twentieth Centuries*. Randall Cherry, trans. New York: Zone Books, 2000.

Fraser, Andrea. *Museum Highlights: The Writings of Andrea Fraser*. Cambridge, MA: MIT Press, 2005.

Freire, Cristina. *Poéticas do Processo: Arte Conceitual no Museu*. São Paulo: Iluminuras, 1999.

_____. *Paulo Bruscky: Arte, Arquivo e Utopia*. São Paulo: Companhia Editora de Pernambuco, 2006.

Grau, Oliver, ed. *Media Art Histories*. Cambridge, MA: MIT Press, 2007.

Fusco, Coco, ed. *Corpus Delecti: Performance Art of the Americas*. New York and London: Routlege, 2000.

Gabeira, Fernando. *O Que É Isso Companheiro*. Rio de Janeiro: Codecri, 1979.

_____. *O Crepúsculo do Macho*. Rio de Janeiro: Codecri, 1980.

Galloway, Alexander R. and Eugene Thacker, eds. *The Exploit: A Theory of Networks*. Minneapolis: University of Minnesota Press, 2007.

Greenstein, M. A. "The Delirium of Faith," *World Art*, No. 3. 1996.

Guattari, Félix. *The Three Ecologies*. London: Athlone Press, 2000.

Guldin, Rainer, "Translation, Self-Translation, Retranslation: Exploring Vilém Flusser's Multilingual Writing Practice" in *Das Spiel mit der Übersetzung. Figuren der Mehrsprachigkeit im Werk Vilém Flussers*, Ranier Guldin, ed., Basel: Tübingen, 2004.

_____. "Iconoclasm and Beyond: Vilém Flusser Concept of Techno-Imagination." *Journal of the Swiss Association of Communication and Media Research*, Vol. 7, N. 2 (2007): 63-84.

Gullar, Ferreira. *Cultura Posta em Questão*. Rio de Janeiro: Civilização Brasileira, 1965.

_____. *Vanguarda e Subdesenvolvimento*. Rio de Janeiro: Civilização Brazileira, 1969.

_____. "Lygia Clark: Uma Experiencia Radical (1954-1958)." In *Lygia Clark*. Rio de Janeiro: Funarte, 1980.

_____. *Etapas da Arte Contemporânea*. São Paulo: Nobel, 1985.

_____. *Toda Poesia*. Rio de Janeiro: José Olympio, 9th Edição, 2000.

Hardt, Michael and Antonio Negri. *Empire*. Cambridge, MA: Harvard University Press, 2000.

Harrison, Charles and Paul Wood, eds. *Art in Theory 1900-2000: An Anthology of Changing Ideas*. Malden, MA: Blackwell, 2003.

Hartog, François. *O Espelho de Heródoto, Ensaio Sobre a Representação do Outro*. Jacyntho Lins Brandão, trans. Belo Horizonte, Brazil: Editora UFMG, 1999.

Harvey, David. *Spaces of Hope*, Robert Hullot-Kentor, trans. Berkeley: University of California Press, 2000.

Heidegger, Martin. *Being and Time*. Joan Stambaugh, trans. Albany: State University of New York Press, 1996.

_____. *What is a Thing?* W. B. Barton, Jr. and Vera Deutsch, trans. Chicago: Henry Regnery Company, 1967.

_____. *The Question Concerning Technology and Other Essays*. William Lovitt, trans. New York: Harper Torchbooks, 1977.

_____. *Basic Writings*. David Farrell Krell, trans. New York: HarperCollins, 1993.

_____. *Introduction to Phenomenological Research*. Daniel O. Dahlstrom, trans. Bloomington: Indiana University Press, 1994.

Hegel, G.W.F. *Phenomenology of the Spirit*. A. V. Miller, trans. Oxford: Clarendon Press, 1977.

Hélio Oiticica, Lygia Clark: Salas Especiais 22 Biennial Internacional de São Paulo. Rio de Janeiro: Museu de Arte Moderna do Rio de Janeiro, 1994.

Herkenhoff, Paulo. "Having Europe for Lunch: A Recipe for Brazilian Art." *Polyester* #2. Spring 1994: 8.

Homem de Mello, Chico, org. *O Design Gráfico Brasileiro Anos 60*. São Paulo: Cosac Naify, 2006.

Jameson, Fredric. *Archaeologies of the Future: The Desire Called Utopia and Other Science Fictions*. New York: Verso, 2005.

Judd, Donald. *Complete Writings 1959–1975*. Halifax, Canada: Press of the Nova Scotia   College of Art and Design, 2005.

Kac, Eduardo, ed. "A Radical Intervention: Brazilian Electronic Art. Documents, Essays and Manifestoes." *Leonardo* <http://leonardo.info/isast/spec.projects/brazil.html>

_____, ed. *Media Poetry: Poetic Innovation and New Technologies*. Bristol: Intellect, 2006. First published as Visible Language 30, No. 2 (1996).

_____, ed. *Signs of Life: Bio Art and Beyond*. Cambridge, MA: MIT Press, 2006.

_____, ed. *Media Poetry: An International Anthology*. Bristol, UK: Intellect, 2007.

_____. *Luz & Letra: Ensaios de Arte, Literatura e Comunicação*. Rio de Janeiro: Contra Capa, 2004.

_____. *Telepresence and Bio Art: Networking Humans, Rabbits, and Robots*. Ann Arbor: University of Michigan Press, 2005.

Kac, Eduardo and Avital Ronell. *Life Extreme: An Illustrated Guide to the New Life*. France: Dis Vois, 2007.

Kalenberg, Ángel. *Eduardo Kac*. Valencia, Spain: IVAM, Institut Valencià D'Art Modern, 2007.

Kepes, Gyorgy, ed. *Structure in Art and in Science*. New York: George Braziller, 1965.

Kosuth, Joseph. *Art after Philosophy and After: Collected Writings, 1996–1990*. Cambridge, MA: MIT Press, 1991.

Kozel, Susan. *Closer: Performance, Technologies, Phenomenology*. Cambridge MA: MIT Press, 2008.

Krause, G. B. *A dúvida de Flusser: filosofia e literatura*. São Paulo: Globo, 2002.

Krause, G. B; Mendes, R., Orgs. *Vilém Flusser no Brasil*. Rio de Janeiro: Relume- Dumará, 2000.

Krauss, Rosalind. *The Originality of the Avant-Garde and Other Modernist Myths*. Cambridge MA: MIT Press, 1985.

_____. *The Optical Unconscious*. Cambridge, MA: The MIT Press, 1993.

_____. *The Originality of the Avant-Garde and Other Modernist Myths*. Cambridge, MA: The MIT Press, 1994.

_____. *Bachelors*. Cambridge, MA: The MIT Press, 1999.

_____. *A Voyage on the North Sea: Art in the Age of the Post-Medium Condition*. New York: Thames & Hudson. 1999.

_____, et al, "Roundtable: The Present Conditions of Art Criticism," *October* 100 (2002): 200–228.

Kristeva, Julia. *The Kristeva Reader*. Toril Moi, ed. New York: Columbia University Press, 1986.

Kunze, Donald. "A Topological Approach to the Uses and Conceptions of Space, in Art, Architecture, and Everyday Life," 2005. Unpublished paper.

Kwinter, Stanford. *Architectures of Time: Toward a Theory of the Event in Modernist Culture*. Cambridge, Mass: The MIT Press, 2002.

Kwon, Miwon. *One Place After Another: Site-Specific Art and Locational Identity*. Cambridge MA: MIT Press, 2002.

Lacan, Jacques. *Écrits*. New York and London: W.W. Norton & Company, 1977.

_____. *The Four Fundamental Concepts of Psycho-Analysis*. Alan Sheridan, trans. New York and London: W.W. Norton & Company, 1981.

Lacoue-Labarthe, Philippe. *A Imitação dos Modernos*. Virginia Figueiredo and J.C. Penna, org. São Paulo: Paz e Terra, 2000.

Latin American Artist of The Twentieth Century. New York: The Museum of Modern Art, 1993.

Latour, Bruno and Peter Weibel, eds. *Iconoclash: Beyond the Image Wars in Science, Religion, and Art*. Karlsruhe: ZKM center for Art and Media, and Cambridge, MA: MIT Press, 2002.

_____, eds., *Iconoclash: Beyond the Image Wars in Science, Religion, and Art*. Karlsruhe, Germany: ZKM Center for Art and Media, and Cambridge, Mass: MIT Press, 2002.

Leeson, Lynn Hershman. "Jaron Lanier Interview," in *Clicking In*. Seattle, WA: Bay Press, 1996.

Leite, Rui Moreira. "Flávio de Carvalho: Media Artist Avant la Lettre." *Leonardo* 37, No. 2 (2004): 150–57.

Lippard, Lucy. *Six Years: The Dematerialization of the Art Object from 1966 to 1972.* Los Angeles: University of California Press, 1997.

Lyotard, Jean-François. *Phenomenology.* Brian Beakley, trans. Albany: State Univ. of New York Press, 1991.

_____. *The Inhuman: Reflections on Time.* Geoffrey Bennington and Rachel Bowlby, trans. Stanford, California: Stanford University Press, 1988.

Machado, Arlindo. "Repensando Flusser e as imagens técnicas." In *O quarto iconoclasmo e outros ensaios hereges.* Rio de Janeiro: Rios Ambiciosos e Contra Capa, 2001.

_____. *Made in Brazil: Três Décadas do Vídeo Brasileiro.* São Paulo: Itaú Cultural, 2003.

MacShine, Kynaston. *The Museum as Muse, Artists Reflect.* New York: The Museum of Modern Art, 1999.

Manovich, Lev. *The Language of New Media.* Cambridge, MA: MIT Press, 2001.

Marks, Laura U. *The Skin of the Film: Intercultural Cinema, Embodiment, and the Senses.* Durham and London: Duke University Press, 2000.

_____. *Touch: Sensuous Theory and Multisensory Media.* Minneapolis-London: University of Minnesota Press, 2002.

McShine, Kynaston L., ed. *Information.* New York: Museum of Modern Art, 1970.

Mendes, Ricardo. "Rumo ao exílio: Vilém Flusser, 1972." Published on the author's web   site: <http://www.fotoplus.com/rico/rmbiocv.htm>

Mendes, Ricardo. *Vilém Flusser: uma história do diabo.* São Paulo: EDUSP, 2001.

Merewether, Charles, ed. *Archives.* Documents of Contemporary Art Series. London: Whitechapel; Cambridge, MA: MIT Press, 2006.

Merleau-Ponty, Maurice. *The visible and the Invisible.* Chicago: Northwestern University Press, 1968.

_____. *Fenomenologia da Percepção.* Rio de Janeiro: Livraria Freitas Bastos, 1971.

Miller, Paul. *Rhythm Science.* Cambridge, MA: MIT Press, 2004.

_____, ed. *Sound Unbound*. Cambridge, MA: MIT Press, 2008.

Milliet, Maria Alice. "A Obra É o Trajeto." In *Revista do MAC #1*. São Paulo: Museu de Arte Contemporânea da Universidade de São Paulo, April 1992.

_____. *Lygia Clark: Obra-Trajeto*. Texto & Arte series #8. São Paulo: Edusp, 1992.

Mirzoeff, Nicholas, ed. *Diaspora and Visual Culture*. London and New York: Routledge, 2000.

Mitchell, W. J. T. *Iconology: Image, Text, Ideology*. Chicago: The University of Chicago Press, 1986.

_____. *Picture Theory*. Chicago: The University of Chicago Press, 1994.

_____. *What do Pictures Want?* Chicago: The University of Chicago Press, 2005.

Mitchell, William J. *The Reconfigured Eye: Visual Truth in the Post-Photographic Era*. Cambridge, MA: The MIT Press, 1992.

Moscatti, Giorgio. "Waldemar Cordeiro Computer Art." originally published as "Arte e Computação: Um Depoimento," *Cadernos MAC-2*. São Paulo (1986): 3-17. Leonardo on-line: http://leonardo.info/ isast/spec.projects/ moscati.html

Mosquera, Gerardo. *Beyond the Fantastic: Contemporary Art and Criticism from Latin America*. Cambridge, MA: MIT Press, 1996.

Mosquera, Gerardo, and Jean Fisher, eds. *Over Here*. Cambridge, MA: MIT Press, 2007.

Nancy, Jean-Luc. *The Birth of Presence*. Stanford, California: Stanford University Press, 1993.

_____. *The Sense of the World*. Feffrey S. Librett, trans. Minneapolis and London: University of Minnesota Press, 1997.

_____. *Being Singular Plural*. Robert D. Richardson and Anne E. O'Byrne, trans. Stanford, California: Stanford University Press, 2000.

Naves, Rodrigo. *A Forma Difícil: Ensaios Sobre Arte Brasileira*. São Paulo: Ática, 1997.

Newman, Amy. *Challenging Art: Artforum 1962-1974*. New York: Soho Press, 2000.

Oiticica Filho, César, Paulo Herkenhoff, and Kátia Maciel, eds. *Cosmococa: Programa in Progress: Hélio Oiticica and Neville D'Almeida*. Rio de Janeiro: Projeto Hélio Oiticica, and Buenos Aires: Centro de Arte Contemporânea Inhotim and Museo de Arte Latinamericano de Buenos Aires, 2005.

Oiticica, Hélio. "Experimentar o Experimental," *Arte em Revista* No. 5. São Paulo: Centro de Estudos de Arte Contemporânea and Kairós, 1981.

Oiticica, Hélio. *Aspiro ao Grando Labirinto*. Rio de Janeiro: Rocco, 1986.

Osthoff, Simone. "Object Lessons," *World Art*, No. 1. 1996: 18-23

_____. "Lygia Clark and Hélio Oiticica: a Legacy of Interactivity and Participation for a Telematic Future." *Leonardo Journal*, Vol. 30, N. 4. (1997): 249-259.

_____. "From Mail Art to Telepresence: Communication at a Distance in the Works of Paulo Bruscky and Eduardo Kac." In *At a Distance: Precursors to Art and Activism on the Internet*. Annmarie Chandler and Norie Neumark, eds. Cambridge, MA: MIT Press, 2005.

_____. "Elsewhere in Contemporary Art: Topologies of Artists' Works, Writings, and Archives," *Art Journal*, VOL. 65, No. 4. (2006): 6-17.

_____. "Eduardo Kac: Networks as Medium and Trope." In *Ecosee*. Sid Dobrin and Sean Morey, eds. Albany: State University of New York Press, 2009.

Pedrosa, Mario. "Significação de Lygia Clark." In *Lygia Clark*. Rio de Janeiro: Funarte, 1980.

Pedrosa, Mario. *Dos Murais de Portinari aos Espaços de Brasília*. São Paulo: Perspectiva, 1981.

Pedrosa, Mario. *Mundo, Homen, Arte em Crise*. São Paulo: Perspectiva, 1986.

Pereira, Maria Antonieta, and Adrian Gorelik. *Das Vanguardas à Brasília*. Belo Horizonte: UFMG, 2005.

Popper, Frank. *Art—Action and Participation*. New York: New York Univ. Press, 1975.

Preziosi, Donald. *Rethinking Art History: Meditations on a Coy Science*. Yale University Press, 1991.

Princenthal, Nancy. "Art Criticism, Bound to Fail." *Art in America*. Jan. 2006: 43–47.

Ramiréz, Marí Carmen and Héctor Olea, eds. *Inverted Utopias: Avant-Garde Art in Latin America*. Houston: Museum of Fine Arts, 2004.

Ramírez, Mari Carmen. "Beyond 'the Fantastic': Framing identity in U.S exhibitions of Latin American Art." *Art Journal* 51. Winter 1992.

_____, org. *Hélio Oiticica: The Body of Color*. Houston, TX and London: Museum of Fine Arts Houston, Texas and the Tate Modern, 2007.

Rancière, Jacques. *The Politics of Aesthetics*. Gabriel Rockhill, trans. New York and London: Continuum, 2004.

_____. *The Future of the Image*. Gregory Elliott, trans. New York: Verso, 2007.

Renov, Michael, ed. *Theorizing Documentary*. New York and London: Routledge, 1993.

Reynolds, Ann. *Robert Smithson: Learning From New Jersey and Elsewhere*. Cambridge, MA: MIT Press, 2003.

Richard, Nelly. "Postmodern Disalignments and Realignments of the Center/Periphery," *Art Journal*, No. 51 (1992).

_____. "Postmodernism and Periphery." In *Postmodernism, A Reader*. Edited by Thomas Doherty. New York: Columbia University Press, 1993.

_____. "The International Mise-en-scéne of Latin American Art." *Witte de With* Cahier #2, 1994.

Rogoff, Irit. *Terra Infirma: Geography's Visual Culture*. London: Routledge, 2000.

_____. "What is a Theorist?" in *The State of Art Criticism*. James Elkins and Michael Newman, eds. The Art Seminar Series Vol. 4. New York and London: Routledge, 2008.

Ronell, Avital. *The Telephone Book: Technology, Schizophrenia, Electric Speech*. University of Nebraska Press, 1991.

_____. *Finitude's Score: Essays for the End of the Millennium*. University of Nebraska Press, 1998

_____. *Stupidity*. Urbana and Chicago: University of Illinois Press, 2002.

_____. *Crack Wars: Literature Addiction Mania.* University of Illinois Press, 2004.

_____. *Dictations: On Haunted Writing.* University of Illinois Press, 2006.

_____. *The Test Drive.* University of Illinois Press, 2007.

_____. *The ÜberReader: Selected Works of Avital Ronell. Diane Davis, ed.* University of Illinois Press, 2007.

Rorty, Richard. *Philosophy and the Mirror of Nature.* Princeton, New Jersey: Princeton University Press, 1979.

Rossi, Elena Giulia, ed. *Eduardo Kac: Move 36.* Paris: Filigranes Editions, 2005.

Rubin, William, ed. *Primitivism in 20th Century Art.* 2 vols. New York: Museum of   Modern Art, 1984.

Rubinstein, Raphael. "A Quiet Crisis." *Art in America.* March 2003: 39–45.

Saramago, José. *Todos os Nomes.* São Paulo: Companhia das Letras, 2003.

Schimmel, Paul, org. *Out of Actions: Between Performances and the Object, 1949- 1979.* Los Angeles: The Museum of Contemporary Art of Los Angeles; and London and New York: Thames and Hudson, 1998.

Schirmacher, Wolfgang. "From the Phenomenon to the Event of Technology" in   *Philosophy and Technology.* F. Rapp. Redel, ed. Boston Studies in the Philosophy of Science 80, 1983.

_____. "Homo Generator: Media and Postmodern Technology." *Culture on the Brink: Ideologies of Technology.* G. Bender and T. Duckrey, eds. New York: The New Press: 1998. Bay Press, 1994.

_____, ed. *German Essays on Science in the 19th Century.* The German Library   36.   New   York   and   London: Continuum, 1996.

_____, ed. *German Essays on Science in the 20th Century.* The German Library 82. New   York   and   London: Continuum, 1996.

_____, ed. *German 20th Century Philosophy: The Frankfurt School.* The German Library 78. New York and London: Continuum, 2000.

_____, ed. *German 20th Century Philosophical Writings.* The

German Library 77. New York and London: Continuum, 2000.

Serres, Michel. *Os Cinco Sentidos: Filosofia dos Corpos Misturados*. Eloá Jacobina, trans. Rio de Janeiro: Editora Bertrand Brazil, 2001.

_____. *The Parasite*. Lawrence R. Schehr, trans. Minneapolis: University of Minnesota Press 2007.

Sharr, Adam. *Heidegger's Hut*. Cambridge, MA: MIT Press, 2006.

Shaw, Jeffrey and Peter Weibel. *Future Cinema: The Cinematic Imaginary After Film*. Karlsruhe: ZKM/ Center for Art and Media; and Cambridge Mass: The MIT Press, 2003.

Smithson, Robert. *The Collected Writings*. Jack Flam, ed. Berkeley: University of California Press, 1996.

Stam, Robert and Ella Shohat. *Subversive Pleasures*. Baltimore: Johns Hopkins University Press, 1989.

Stam, Robert and Ella Shohat. *Unthinking Eurocentrism*. New York: Routledge, 1994.

Ströl, Andréas, ed. *Vilém Flusser Writings*. Erik Eisel, trans. Minneapolis: University of Minnesota Press, 2002.

Sullivan, Edward. *Brazil Body and Soul*. New York and Bilbao: Guggenheim Museum, 2001.

Taquini, Graciela. *Eduardo Kac: Obras Vivas y en Red, Fotografías y Otros Trabajos*. Buenos Aires, Argentina: Fundación Telefonica, 2006.

Taylor, Diana. *The Archive and the Repertoire*. Durham & London: Duke University Press, 2003.

Thompson, Robert Farris. *The Face of the Gods*. New York: The Museum of African Art, 1993.

Ulmer, Gregory. *Applied Grammatology: Post(e)-Pedagogy from Jacques Derrida to Joseph Beuys (E-Pedagogy from Jacques Derrida to Joseph Beuys)*. Baltimore: The Johns Hopkins University Press, 1984.

_____. "The Miranda Warnings: An Experiment in Hyperrhetoric." In *Hyper/Text/Theory*. George Landow, ed. Baltimore: Johns Hopkins University Press, 1994.

_____. "The Object of Post-Criticism." *The Anti-Aesthetic*. Hal Foster, ed. Seattle: Bay Press, 1983.

202 Performing the Archive

Ventura, Zuenir. *1968 O Ano que Não Terminou.* Rio de Janeiro: Nova Fronteira, 1988.

_____. *Cidade Partida.* Rio de Janeiro: Companhia das Letras, 1994.

Verger, Pierre Fatumbi. *Orixás.* Salvador, Bahia: Currupio, 1981.

Vesna, Victoria, ed. *Database Aesthetics: Art in the Age of Information Overflow.* Minneapolis: University of Minnesota Press, 2007.

Weibel, Peter. "An End to the 'End of Art'? On the Iconoclasm of Modern Art." in *Iconoclash: Beyond the Image Wards in Science, Religion,* Bruno Latour and Art, Peter Weibel, eds. Cambridge, MA and Karlsruhe, Germany: The MIT Press and AKM Center for Art and Media, 2002.

Weintraub, Linda. *In The Making.* New York: d.a.p., 2003.

White, Hayden. *Metahistory: The Historical Imagination in Nineteenth-Century Europe.* Baltimore: The Johns Hopkins University Press, 1973.

Yates, Francis. *The Art of Memory.* Chicago: University of Chicago Press, 2001.

Zegher, M. Catherine de. org. *Inside the Visible: An Eliptical Traverse of 20th Century Art.* Boston and Cambridge: Museum of Contemporary Art and MIT Press, 1996.

Zelevansky, Lynn, ed. *Beyond Geometry: Experiments in Form 1940s-70s,* at LACMA, Los Angeles County Museum of Art, 2004.

Zielinski, Siegfried. *Audiovisions: Cinema and Television as Entr'actes in History.* Amsterdam: Amsterdam University Press, 1999.

_____. *Deep Time of the Media: Towards an Archeology of Hearing and Seeing Through Technical Means.* Cambridge, MA: MIT Press, 2006.

Zizek, Slavoj. *The Sublime Object of Ideology.* New York: Verso, 1989.

_____. *Tarrying with the Negative, Kant, Hegel, and the Critique of Ideology.* Durham: Duke University Press, 1993.

_____. *The Plague of Fantasies.* New York: Verso, 1997.

_____. *The Ticklish Subject, the absent centre of political ontology*. New York: Verso, 1999.

_____. *Looking Awry, An Introduction to Jacques Lacan Through Popular Culture*. Cambridge, MA: MIT Press, 1997.

_____. *The Parallax View*. Cambridge, MA: MIT Press, 2006.

Think Media: EGS Media Philosophy Series

Wolfgang Schirmacher, editor

The Ethics of Uncertainty: Aporetic Openings. Michael Anker

Trans/actions: Art, Film and Death. Bruce Alistair Barber

Trauma, Hysteria, Philosophy. Hannes Charen and Sarah Kamens

Literature as Pure Mediality: Kafka and the Scene of Writing.
Paul DeNicola

Deleuze and the Sign. Christopher M. Drohan

Imaginality: Conversant and Eschaton. A. Staley Groves

Hospitality in the age of media representation. by Christian Hänggi

**The Organic Organisation: freedom, creativity and
the search for fulfilment.** Nicholas Ind

Media Courage: impossible pedagogy in an artificial community.
Fred Isseks

Mirrors triptych technology: Remediation and Translation Figures.
Diana Silberman Keller

Sonic Soma: Sound, Body and the Origins of the Alphabet.
Elise Kermani

**The Art of the Transpersonal Self: Transformation as Aesthetic and Energetic
Practice.** Norbert Koppensteiner

Can Computers Create Art? James Morris

Propaganda of the Dead: Terrorism and Revolution. Mark Reilly.

The Novel Imagery: Aesthetic Response as Feral Laboratory. Dawan Stanford.

Community without Identity: The Ontology and Politics of Heidegger.
Tony See

—*other books available from Atropos Press*

Teletheory. Gregory L. Ulmer

Philosophy of Culture-Kulturphilosophie: Schopenhauer and Tradition. Edited by
Wolfgang Schirmacher.

Grey Ecology. Paul Virilio
Edited with introduction by Hubertus von Amelunxen. Translated by Drew Burk

Talking Cheddo: Liberating PanAfrikanism. Menkowra Manga Clem Marshall

The Tupperware Blitzkrieg. Anthony Metivier

Che Guevara and the Economic Debate in Cuba. Luiz Bernardo Pericás

Follow Us or Die. Vincent W.J. van Gerven Oei and Jonas Staal

Just Living: Philosophy in Artificial Life. Collected Works Volume 1.
Wolfgang Schirmacher

Lightning Source UK Ltd.
Milton Keynes UK
UKHW01f1829050718
325294UK00001B/91/P